30.00

AF814120

This is the earliest known drawing of Santa Barbara done in 1793 by John Sykes, a member of the George Vancouver expedition. It shows the Indian village "Syuhtun" at the beach, with the Presidio and Mission in the background. Courtesy Hydrographer of the Navy, Taunton, England

The Santa Barbara News-Press,
at 134 years the oldest daily
newspaper in Southern California,
is proud to sponsor
this limited edition of

Santa Barbara:
Historical Themes and Images.

SANTA BARBARA

Historical Themes & Images

by JARRELL C. JACKMAN

Design by Sharon Varner Moyer

THE
DONNING COMPANY
PUBLISHERS
NORFOLK/VIRGINIA BEACH

This book is dedicated
to
Michele Jackman,
the world's greatest living wife,
and
Wallace Stegner,
America's greatest living author.

For information, write:

The Donning Company/Publishers
5659 Virginia Beach Boulevard
Norfolk, Virginia 23502

Edited by Beverley Hainer
Richard A. Horwege, Senior Editor

Library of Congress Cataloging-in-Publication Data:

Jackman, Jarrell C.
Santa Barbara: historical themes and images
by Jarrell C. Jackman.

p. cm.
Bibliography: p.
Includes index.
ISBN 0-89865-739-3

1. Santa Barbara (Calif.)—History—Pictorial works.
2. Santa Barbara (Calif.)—Description—Views. I. Title.
F869-S45J33 1988 88-25649
979.4'91—dc 19 CIP

Printed in the United States of America

Contents

Foreword

That one-time friend of Santa Barbara, Will Rogers, once remarked that he knew only what he read in newspapers. It is true that newspapers record an instant history of their communities every day. But often lost in the swirl of events, in the hectic here-and-now, is a sense of perspective. As a newspaper editor I readily confess we are often too bound by daily deadlines to separate the lasting from ephemeral.

The task of the historian is to offer that perspective, to provide an evaluation tempered by time and balanced by knowledge. Santa Barbara's complex and, at times, controversial history requires a skilled interpreter. So we are fortunate that Jarrell Jackman, a scholar, historian, and citizen of Santa Barbara, has turned his talents to exploring and illuminating this community's past.

In Dr. Jackman's concise and graceful text, and in the striking images of this book, many taken from the photographic files of the *News-Press*, we are witness to the story of Santa Barbara. And, in the end, we are enlightened about the history of this land, sheltered between the mountains and the sea, and we discover its lasting attraction.

B. Dale Davis
Editor and Publisher
Santa Barbara News-Press

Santa Barbara, California
August 1, 1988

Preface

Santa Barbara and the surrounding region have a rich and complex history. Choosing some three hundred and fifty images representative of that history is a daunting task. It throws the historian back on his own wits and makes him aware of his personal biases. I hope the reader shares some of these biases and that justice is done to Santa Barbara history.

Each chapter in this book uses history as a tool for understanding the world in which we live. The thread that weaves our experiences together is our cultural heritage, which I would define in the broadest sense as the sum of our activities—the arts, technology, educational systems, politics, and the like.

The historical themes explored here reveal the "connectedness of all things." A link exists between the early Chumash and the way we live today, between the Chicano and Spanish heritages, between the Old Spanish Days and Solstice parades, between the authors Stewart Edward White and Ross Macdonald, between an eighteenth century leather-jacket soldier and a Vandenberg rocket soaring into space.

In present-day Santa Barbara we are witnessing enormous physical and technological changes, and Los Angeles is knocking on our door, but there is an underlying, unconscious whisper speaking to us from the past.

Listen to it carefully; in it we may find redemption.

Acknowledgments

First and foremost, I wish to thank Jeff Flanders, Vice-President of the Santa Barbara *News-Press*, who asked me to undertake this book and whose cooperation throughout the project has helped bring it to fruition. Jeff and Publisher B. Dale Davis gave me complete and open access to the *News-Press* photo collection and clipping files. A special thanks also to Sue De Lapa, *News-Press* librarian and loyal volunteer of the Santa Barbara Trust for Historic Preservation, for her willingness to assist me in my research in any way she could.

Roseanne Barker of the University of California at Santa Barbara Library Department of Special Collections went well beyond the call of duty retrieving photos from the Pearl Chase Collection and patiently answering my many phone inquiries. I thank, too, Chris Brun for granting me permission to use photos from the Department of Special Collections.

Susan Dixon, librarian at the Museum of Natural History, was very helpful finding material for me on John Peabody Harrington, one of my heroes. Speaking of heroes, I have the deepest respect for John Johnson, curator at the Museum of Natural History, who is incredibly knowledgeable on the Chumash. Every time I called him, he was most accommodating in responding to my queries.

At the Historical Society, librarian Mike Redmon, a former student of mine at the University of California at Santa Barbara, is the epitome of good will and good service. We had many interesting conversations about Santa Barbara history during my frequent visits to the Gledhill Library. I am also grateful to Richard Esparza, executive director of the Society, for showing me the Henry Ford Chapman painting in his office that is on the dust jacket of this book.

Linda Moore, my assistant at the Trust for Historic Preservation, and Cathy Rudolph, Presidio archivist, both made valuable suggestions for improving the manuscript. Linda also tracked down photos and ably assisted me in countless other ways. The rest of the Trust staffers—Phyllis Moore, Kerry Marcu, Fritzie Seidler and Guy Wilson—have also earned my generous appreciation for putting up with my grousing over the past year.

My gratitude also goes to my long-time friend Patrick O'Dowd, who loves the world of ideas and has a unique way of stimulating one's creative instincts. I would be remiss if I did not mention talented photographer William Dewey who was thorough and prompt in the work he did for me.

I also want to thank the many people who came forward with photos from their family or private collections and who generously let me use these photos in the book.

Last but hardly least my wife, Michele, and daughter, Renee, have provided an enormous amount of support and encouragement, especially at times when I was sure waves of exhaustion were going to overcome me.

While I am indebted to all of the people above, I alone am responsible for any errors or flaws the reader may discover.

In the nineteenth century two Indians stood before the Santa Barbara Mission. The purpose of the Mission system was to save souls and prepare the Indians for civilization. But European diseases interceded and thousands of Chumash succumbed. The adobe building by the fence was near the area where the Chumash were housed. Courtesy Santa Barbara Historical Society

Before the arrival of the Spanish, Santa Barbara was the most densely populated Indian region in California. Population estimates at the time of European contact range between fifteen thousand and seventeen thousand. This map drawn by anthropologist John Johnson shows the Chumash settlements along the central coast at the time of Spanish colonization in the eighteenth century. Map courtesy John Johnson

Chapter One

The Chumash

Just slightly over two hundred years ago, a native people we today call "the Chumash" were Santa Barbara's sole human inhabitants. Residents in the region for thousands of years, the Chumash went into rapid decline after the arrival of the first Spanish colonizers. Thus it is only possible to conjure up in the mind's eye what these people were like in prehistoric times.

The Chumash woman normally wore a buckskin skirt, the edges of which were cut in fringes and ornamented with strings of beads and shells. Waist-up, she was clad in winter in a pullover made of fox or rabbit skin. Her hair was trimmed in short bangs and left hanging down neatly and gracefully over her back. Her husband, often naked, had his nose and ears pierced with containers filled with wild tobacco powder; his hair was interwoven with bone, flint, and wood. He stood alert and agile. In cold weather he donned a long skin coat.

He, his wife, and children lived in one of the many villages in the region. In their daily lives, they ate plants and nuts, as well as the fish and fresh meat available. They made intricate baskets, painted on the walls of caves, and built elaborate canoes; were involved in trade with the islands and areas outside of Santa Barbara, sang songs, played musical instruments, and had a complex religion. Believing that religious ceremonies were needed to balance the forces of nature, they celebrated the winter solstice "to pull the sun back to the earth."

Then came the turning point for the Chumash in the 1770s when Spanish Governor Felipe de Neve and Fray Junipero Serra debated over what should be done with the Indians. De Neve felt they should be allowed to stay in their villages. Serra insisted they had to be brought to the missions. Serra prevailed, with the result that by 1805 all of the coastal Chumash villages had been abandoned. As the nineteenth century progressed, the Chumash and their heritage began to slip away. Only a few native speakers survived in 1912 when anthropologist John Peabody Harrington, a Santa Barbara High School and Phi Beta Kappa Stanford graduate, began interviewing Chumash informants. Over the course of fifty years, Harrington recorded page after page of notes on the Chumash. This man almost singlehandedly kept alive the flickering flame of this dying culture.

The more than 300,000 pages of notes Harrington left behind have become the fertile soil out of which a Chumash rebirth has emerged. The spiritual power of these people should not be underestimated, for their message is pertinent to us today. We are not at peace in or with this Edenic land. Part of our problem is that we have demystified nature. It has become an inanimate object to be exploited. The Chumash of the past tell us that our technological genius must be brought into harmony with the Chumash way. According to their

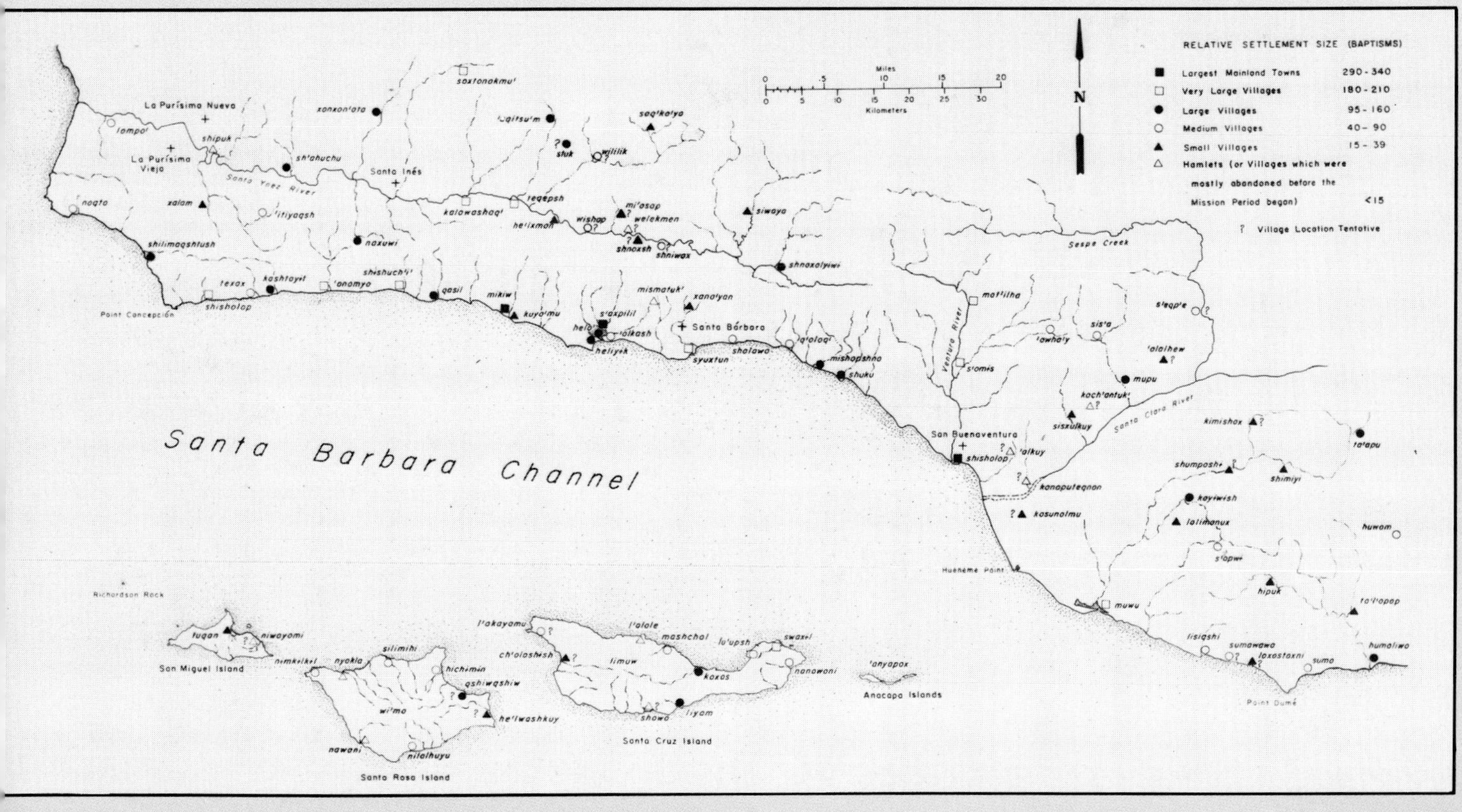

belief, the wind is the "breath of the world," the means by which the earth and the human connect with one another. We must re-establish that connection.

Every person who wants to contribute to the betterment of life in Santa Barbara must begin with a study of the Chumash, must have a sense of their legacy. As long as we ignore them, we run the danger of floundering.

An artist's rendering re-creates what Mescalitan Island and Goleta Slough may have looked like in prehistoric times. Courtesy Santa Barbara Bank & Trust

Once an island in an estuary, Mescalitan contained a Chumash village in prehistoric times. Along the rim of the inlet were other Chumash villages. Most of the estuary silted in in the nineteenth century and the island was bulldozed, except for a small piece which is today the site of a sewage treatment plant. In the 1940s dirt from the area was used as fill for the airport. This photograph of the island was taken over fifty years ago. To the right is the site of present-day Goleta Beach. Courtesy Santa Barbara Trust for Historic Preservation

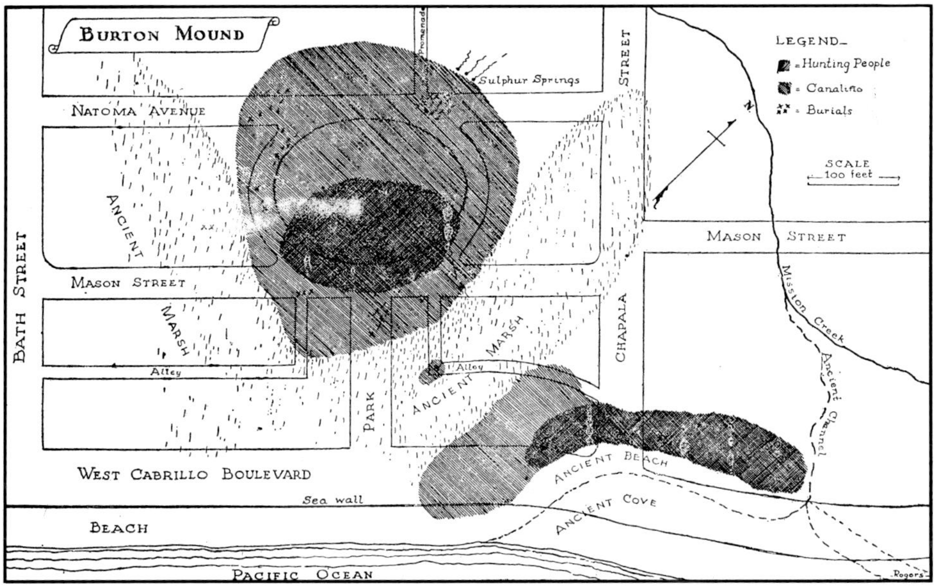

Burton Mound, receiving its name from the settler who lived there in the nineteenth century, was an ancient village site (Syuhtun) occupied by the Chumash when the Spanish arrived in 1782. The mound, a giant Chumash midden (i.e., trash heap), was excavated in the twentieth century by anthropologist John P. Harrington and other archaeologists. The famous Potter Hotel was built on the site. Drawing courtesy Santa Barbara News-Press

Burton Mound once stood at the end of the row of palm trees in this photo taken from West Cabrillo Boulevard. The land still rises at the apartment complex and surrounding area. Courtesy Santa Barbara News-Press

Rafael Solares, Chumash Capitan at Zanja de Cota (today the Santa Ynez Reservation), posed for these photos taken by Leon de Cessac in 1878. The dress is authentic Chumash. Courtesy Musee de L'Homme, Paris

Rafael Solares is shown flint knapping (i.e., making projectile points). Courtesy Musee de L'Homme, Paris

This Chumash conical hut was reconstructed at Mission La Purisima near Lompoc. Made from willow poles and layered from bottom up with tule (bulrush or cattails), the huts were eighteen to twenty feet high and sometimes as large as thirty-five feet across. Courtesy Santa Barbara News-Press

Unidentified individuals, probably some of them of Chumash descent, stood in front of a conical hut under construction at the Ventura County Fair in 1923. Courtesy Smithsonian Institution

Painted Cave, one of the best examples of the rich Chumash rock art found in the Santa Ynez mountains, is maintained and protected by the California Department of Parks and Recreation. What do the colorful designs and configurations mean? Anthropologists have been pondering this question for years and posited various theories, any one of which is as true as the other. Courtesy Santa Barbara Museum of Natural History

Campbell Grant, a local artist and teacher, has spent a lifetime drawing, photographing, and studying Chumash cave drawings. The rock art of the Chumash is considered the finest found in North America. Photo Courtesy Santa Barbara News-Press

The "Tomol," an oceangoing plank canoe, was a unique creation of the Chumash. The boats, made of pine wood and fashioned with stone tools, took about forty days to build. Sometimes redwood drifting down from the north was used. Logs were split into planks and smoothed with sharkskin sandpaper to fit snugly. The planks were then tied with rope made from milkweed, painted, decorated with shells, and finally sealed with tar. They were thirty feet long and were used to cross the channel or fish offshore. Courtesy Santa Barbara Museum of Natural History

In 1976 Indians paddled near Ortega Hill in an authentic replica built under the direction of Peter Howorth and Travis Hudson. The boat is on display in the Natural History Museum. Courtesy Santa Barbara Museum of Natural History

One anthropologist has written: "In workmanship and design, Chumash basketry ranks among the finest in North America." Photos courtesy University of California, Santa Barbara

For the Chumash, the condor was a sacred creature; for modern man, he is another victim facing extinction. Mystery writer Ross Macdonald said it best: "The condor is our canary in the mine. If he survives, perhaps we will too." Courtesy Santa Barbara News-Press

John P. Harrington (1884-1961) was photographed posing in a grass skirt. A graduate of Santa Barbara High School, Harrington may be the most important historical personage in Santa Barbara in the twentieth century. He spent countless hours recording the vanishing Chumash language and culture as an ethnologist working for the Smithsonian Institution. He took down over 300,000 pages of notes from interviews with Chumash Indians in the Santa Barbara and Ventura region. A gifted linguist, he has been called our nation's greatest ethnographer. His efforts have contributed to the revival of Chumash culture among various local Indian groups. Courtesy Smithsonian Institution

Harrington spent his retirement years at the Riviera Hotel on Carrillo Street (next to the present-day fire department), where he continued to work on his notes. He died in San Diego, having returned there to be with his daughter. Courtesy Santa Barbara Historical Society

John P. Harrington's first consultant was Fernando Librado, a Chumash, who posed for this photograph in 1913. Born at Mission San Buenaventura, Librado died in Santa Barbara. Courtesy Smithsonian Institution

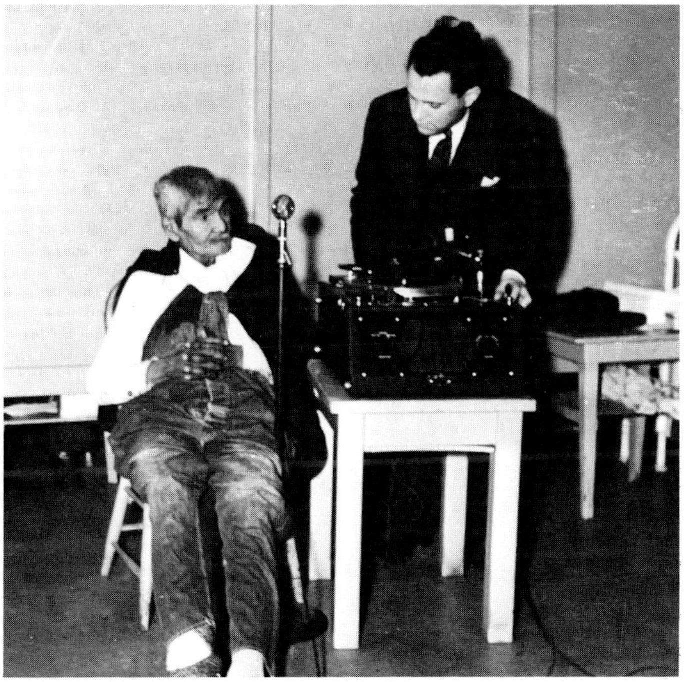

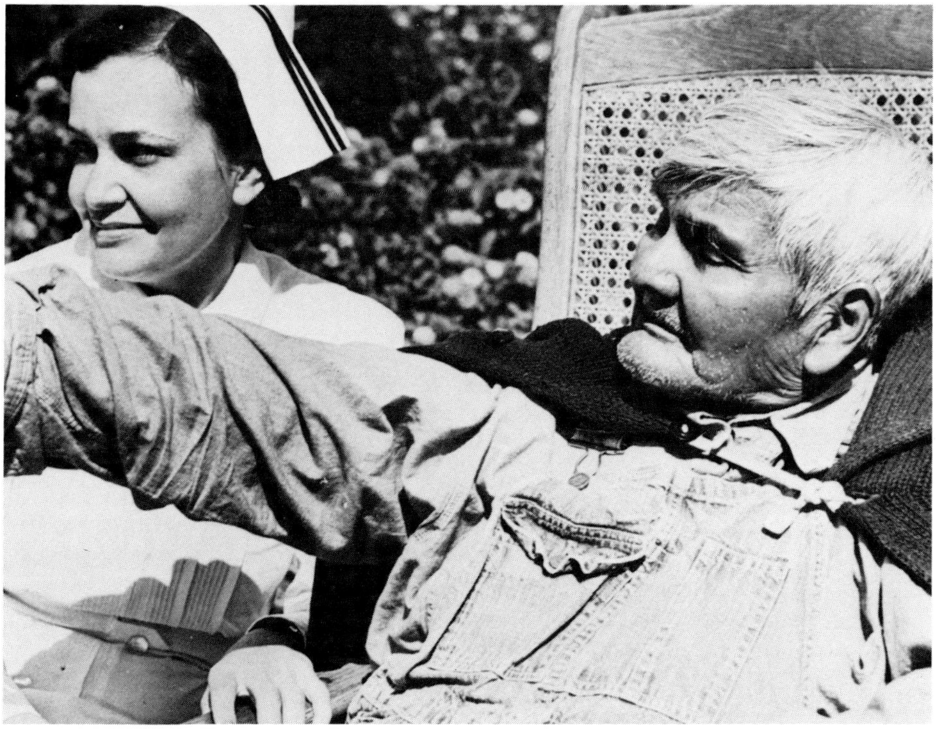

Juan Justo was photographed at Santa Barbara County Hospital shortly before his death in 1941. He was interviewed by Harrington's nephew, Arthur Harrington, and was one of the last native speakers. Courtesy Santa Barbara Historical Society

Lucrecia Garcia (1877-1937), also interviewed extensively by Harrington, was the mother of Mary Yee, the last surviving Indian to speak fluent Barbareño Chumash. Courtesy Santa Barbara National History Museum

Ernestine McGovran, daughter of Mary Yee, hopes some day to be able to translate her mother's journals. Courtesy Santa Barbara News-Press

Mary Yee (1897-1966), shown in this circa 1920 photo, was the last native speaker of Barbareño Chumash. Courtesy Ernestine McGovran

In 1978 Indians protested against construction of a proposed LNG plant at Point Conception on a sacred Chumash religious site. The plant was never built. Much of native American activity recently has been political in nature, an attempt to restore Chumash dignity and culture to their rightful place in modern Santa Barbara. Courtesy Santa Barbara News-Press

Crane Dancer of the Santa Ynez Reservation performs in the street at Presidio Days, celebrated April 21 through 24, 1988. According to Fernando Librado, Chumash danced in front of the Presidio chapel during the Hispanic period. Photo by Guy Wilson

Juan Rodriguez Cabrillo, sailing under the flag of Spain, entered the Santa Barbara channel in 1542 with his two ships, thereby becoming the first European to see the south coast. Cabrillo survived serving under Cortez in Mexico and on forays in Guatemala. But off Santa Barbara his luck ran out. Breaking his arm in a freak accident, he died from the injury and is thought to be buried on San Miguel Island. A recent biography of Cabrillo, however, has suggested that the explorer may actually have been buried on Catalina Island, although the evidence is by no means conclusive. A monument in Cabrillo's memory has been erected on San Miguel. Courtesy Santa Barbara News-Press

Chapter Two

The Spirit of 1782

Charles Fletcher Lummis (1859-1928)—a long-time Southern California resident, who during his lifetime was editor of the Los Angeles *Times*, Los Angeles City Librarian, author, and founder of the Landmarks Club (1897) and the Southwest Museum (1914)—had a strong interest in and respect for both the Indians and Spanish pioneers of California. After a visit to Santa Barbara, Lummis wrote that the town should "stand fast" in preserving its Spanish heritage and architecture. Santa Barbara has taken to heart Lummis's clarion call and, perhaps more than any other community in California, has embraced its early Hispanic history. Let us call this the "Spirit of 1782," in honor of the year the town was founded by Governor Felipe de Neve, Father Serra, and the Spanish soldiers and families who accompanied them.

Until recently historical research on early California has overemphasized the missions and the mission system, to the neglect of the Spanish civilian and military history of the period. Further, many of the writers who have taken up the subject have tended to romanticize the Spanish and Mexican eras and in the process angered many Indians who in turn have lashed out at the mission system for the destruction it wrought on native California peoples.

Santa Barbarans have viewed their early history with their own fair share of romanticism, perhaps best symbolized by the huge murals in the county courthouse that portray Santa Barbara's Spanish heroes as literally bigger than life. The Old Mission, the city's signature landmark, also evokes in its silent beauty a feeling of romanticism. Today, there is a tendency to tell it like it really was, not how we wish it had been. The fact remains that the early explorers (Cabrillo, Vizcaino, Portola and De Anza) were intrepid fellows and cut romantic figures. One also cannot but admire the commitment and courage of the padres who went to live among the Indians, hoping to bring them salvation and the benefits of civilization. The Franciscans were not the first people to believe they were doing the right thing, only to have subsequent generations view their efforts as misguided.

There are those, too, who think that Santa Barbara's obsession with its Spanish past is misguided. To these people it is truly quixotic that the Santa Barbara Trust for Historic Preservation is attempting to rebuild an old Spanish adobe fort in the middle of the city on a site partially covered with structures from a later period. The Presidio advocates plow ahead relentlessly, feeling assured that what they are doing is of great historical significance, that the history revealed will deepen the public's respect for the Spanish and Mexican roots of Santa Barbara. They feel, too, that the simple, basic existence of the eighteenth century on display at El Presidio de Santa Barbara State Historic Park will provide a vivid contrast to the modern hustle and bustle of the city around it. They know that no other development in town is going to create open space, reduce water use, and teach its populace how to build adobe buildings that literally spring from the soil. They are aware that no other project will help shatter the myth of the early colonists as conquistadors and demonstrate that the soldiers and families who settled in Santa Barbara were a mixture of people, including full-blooded Indians, mestizos, and mulattos from Baja California, Sonora, and Sinaloa, Mexico.

The Presidio project is only one aspect of "The Spirit of 1782," albeit one of the most noble. It can be seen in the few old adobes that survive around town, in the twentieth century rebuilding of the city in Hispanic style of architecture, in the descendants who search out their family histories, and in those individuals who continue to participate in Old Spanish Days celebrations. Without a doubt, Santa Barbara's Hispanic heritage is a powerful force that, if tempered with a deeper understanding of its culturally diverse origins, will continue to energize our community for many years to come.

Three Spanish frigates under Sebestian Vizcaino entered the Santa Barbara Channel in 1602. It was the custom of the padre on the expedition to name new localities in honor of the saint on whose festival day the discovery took place. December 4 is the feast day of Saint Barbara, who in the third century A.D. was locked in a tower and then decapitated by her Roman father for her unrepented Christian beliefs. This beautiful painting of Saint Barbara was done by Jose de Alcibar in Mexico in 1783 and arrived in Santa Barbara in 1787. It hangs in the Presidio Chapel. Photo by William Dewey

Carlos III, king of Spain when Santa Barbara was founded in 1782, is commemorated by this statue in the plazuela next to the News-Press *building facing State Street. The casting is one of two originals by the eighteenth century sculptor Alfonso G. Bergaz. Photo by Rafael Maldonado; Courtesy Santa Barbara* News-Press

On their trek through California in 1769-70, Gasper de Portolá and the other members of his "Sacred Expedition" became the first Europeans to travel by land over the Santa Barbara region. In 1776, the De Anza expedition, comprising 240 colonists, also passed through Santa Barbara on its way to San Francisco. This famous expedition was reenacted in 1976, with history enthusiasts participating from as far away as Arizona. Santa Barbarans also participated in the reenactment as seen in this rehearsal in Hope Ranch. The 1776 expedition started in Horcasitas, Mexico, crossing over rugged desert terrain with only one person dying along the way. Courtesy George and Vivian Obern

Santa Barbara was founded on April 21, 1782, by a group of soldiers and their families led by Governor Felipe de Neve, Fray Junipero Serra and the first Presidio comandante *Jose Francisco Ortega. In 1982 the founding of the Presidio, the city's birthplace, was reenacted in a ceremony similar to that of two hundred years before. A cross was raised, a simple song called the "Alabado" sung, and a Mass celebrated. Russell Clay Ruiz, a Presidio descendant, dressed in the dark uniform, is standing to the right of the cross. Courtesy Santa Barbara Trust for Historic Preservation*

Seen here is the Santa Barbara Presidio in the 1790s as envisioned by artist and Presidio descendant Russell Antonio Ruiz. Courtesy Santa Barbara Historical Society

The Spanish Presidio (or fort) consisted of whitewashed adobe buildings with red-tiled roofs. El Cuartel, shown here in the nineteenth century, was once a quarters shared by a soldier and his family. Courtesy Santa Barbara Trust for Historic Preservation

A California Presidio soldier, 1791, wearing his cuera blanca *(white leather jacket) after a sketch made by Jose Cardero. Courtesy Harry and Ellen Knill of Bellerophon Books*

A California soldier's wife, after Cardero: she wears an enagua, *or transparent muslin skirt and pearls from Baja California; a tight-fitting silk blouse joins the skirt. Her shoes,* zapatos de patillo, *had high wooden heels. A silk* rebozo *or shawl was also worn. Courtesy Harry and Ellen Knill*

In 1963, the Santa Barbara Trust for Historic Preservation was formed with the primary goal of reconstructing the Presidio. In 1963 El Cuartel was acquired by the Trust and later donated to the State of California becoming the nucleus of El Presidio de Santa Barbara State Historic Park. Constructed in 1788, El Cuartel is the oldest building owned by the state and the oldest surviving building in Santa Barbara County. Courtesy Santa Barbara Trust for Historic Preservation

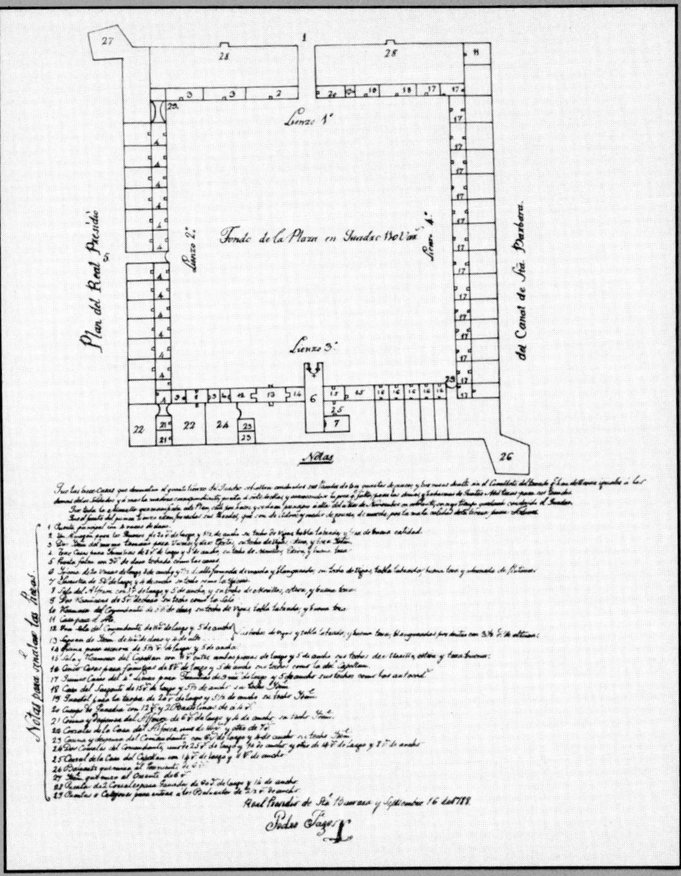

This 1788 ground plan of the Santa Barbara Presidio signed by Spanish Governor Pedro Fages is one of the most important surviving documents of early California history. The plan describes construction materials, the size of rooms, and how each room was used. Its accuracy has been confirmed by archaeological work at the site. Map courtesy Newberry Library, Chicago

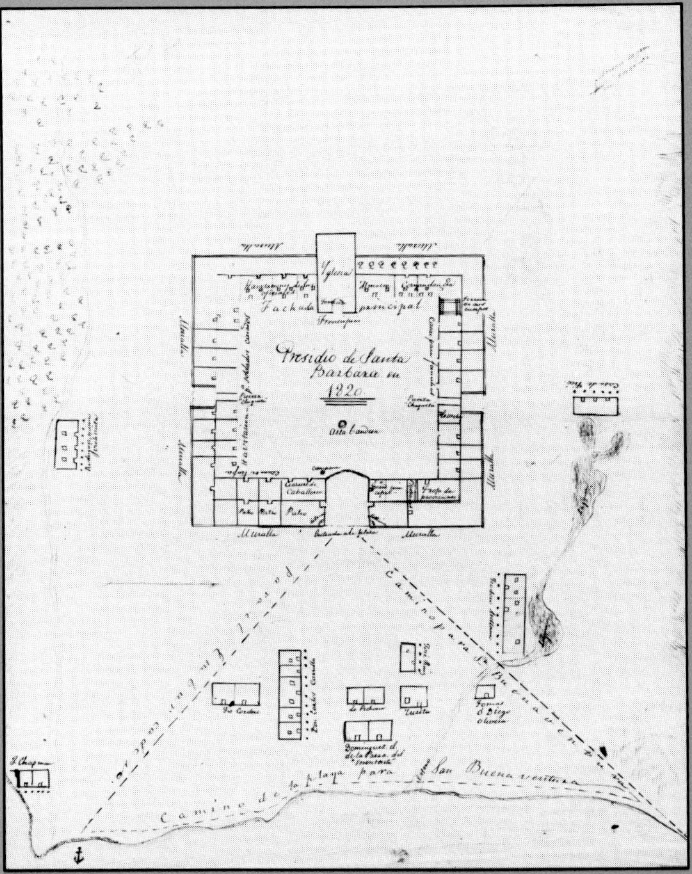

This 1820 map of the Santa Barbara Presidio was rediscovered in the Bancroft Library (Berkeley) in 1982, along with maps of the other three Spanish California fortresses. The map, while less detailed than the Fages plan, has provided new information for the Presidio reconstruction, most notably evidence that a bell tower had been constructed and that a two-story observation tower existed near the commandant's quarters. Courtesy Bancroft Library, U. C. Berkeley

A number of people have contributed to the Presidio project over the years including among others, Pearl Chase, Jeremy Hass, and Mary Louise Days, but none gave more than Russell Antonio Ruiz, (1926-1988), a Presidio descendant shown in this photograph with his paintings in the background. Ruiz spent a lifetime researching and writing about the Spanish period in Santa Barbara. Courtesy Santa Barbara News-Press

In 1969 upon retiring as Santa Barbara County Planning Director, Richard Whitehead (1907-1988) became actively involved with the Trust for Historic Preservation and began collecting research materials on the Presidio that now form the basis of the newly established Presidio Research Center. Russell Ruiz and Whitehead embody the "Spirit of 1782" that has held sway over Santa Barbara for the past two hundred years. Photo by William Dewey

Norman Neuerburg, one of the most gifted art historians in the nation and a leading authority on the Spanish period in California, researched, designed, and executed the interior for the Santa Barbara Presidio Chapel reconstruction. This Hollywood High and UCLA graduate was also historical consultant for the design of the Getty Museum in Malibu. Courtesy Santa Barbara News-Press

An 1855 water color by Lt. James Alden shows the Presidio chapel a few years before it was destroyed by an earthquake. Courtesy Santa Barbara Mission Archive Library

The only surviving remnants of the original Presidio chapel in 1982 were these foundations. The reconstructed padre's quarters is seen in the background. Courtesy Santa Barbara Trust for Historic Preservation

After years of research and archaeology, reconstruction of the chapel began in 1981 with the production of adobe bricks at the Old Mission. California Conservation Corps members provided the labor. Courtesy Santa Barbara Trust for Historic Preservation

Thirty-thousand bricks were needed for the chapel, about 90 percent of which were made by the California Conservation Corps. The remaining 10 percent were made by volunteers. Courtesy Santa Barbara News-Press

California Conservation Corps member Laura Finney lifts adobe mortar during the chapel reconstruction in 1983. Photo by Steve Malone; Courtesy Santa Barbara News-Press

Volunteers, shown whitewashing the Presidio chapel, have been instrumental throughout the history of the project. Courtesy Santa Barbara Trust for Historic Preservation

CCC *interns Ralph Ross (left) and Marlon Moland in front of the reconstructed chapel. Photo by Bob Ponce; Courtesy Santa Barbara* News-Press

An archaeological miracle took place in 1983, when this Presidio period tile floor was discovered intact beneath two modern structures by archaeologist Vance Bente and UCSB students. Courtesy Santa Barbara News-Press

A section of the Presidio aqueduct was uncovered during a 1988 phase of archaeology. It may have been in use as early as 1784. Photo by William Dewey

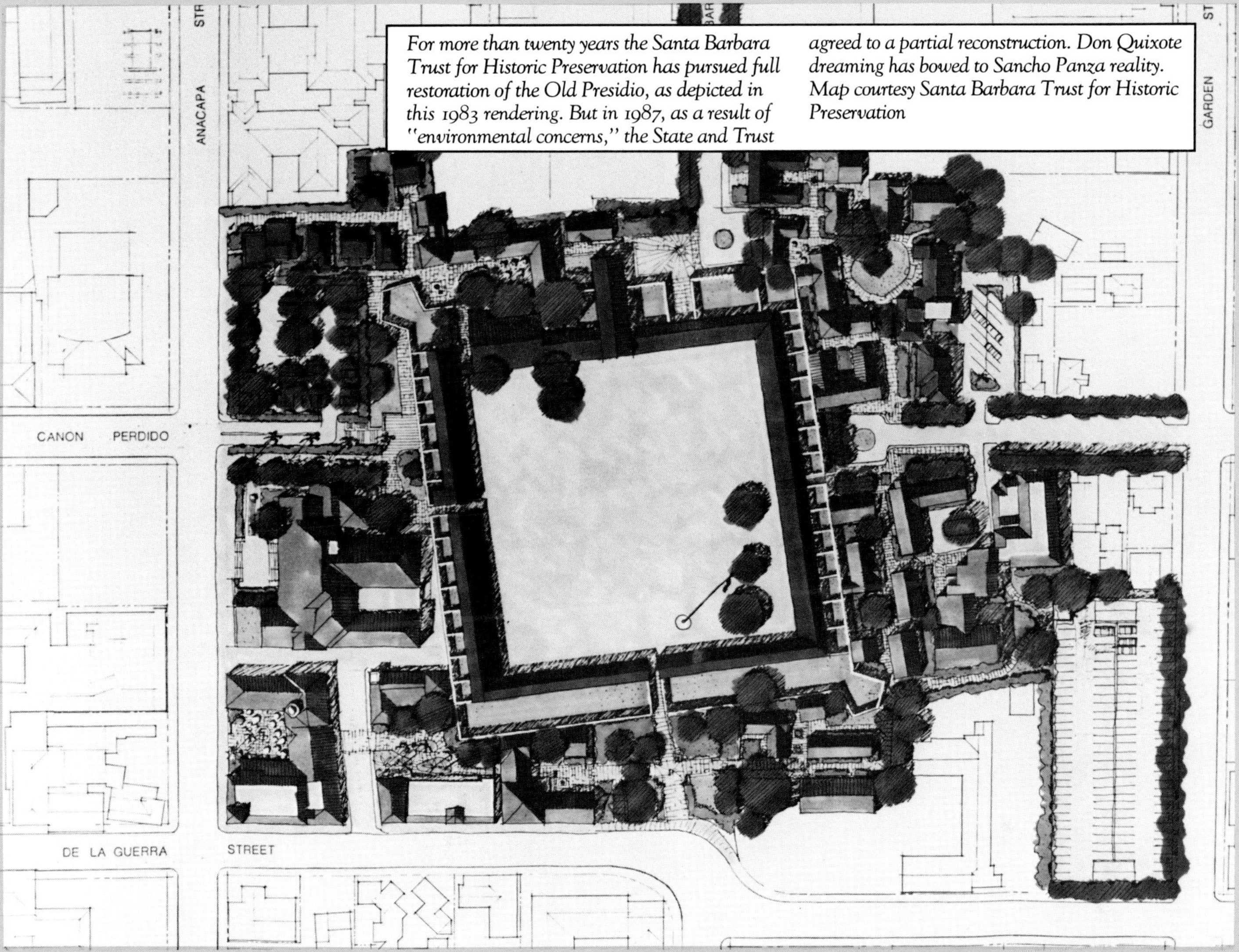

For more than twenty years the Santa Barbara Trust for Historic Preservation has pursued full restoration of the Old Presidio, as depicted in this 1983 rendering. But in 1987, as a result of "environmental concerns," the State and Trust agreed to a partial reconstruction. Don Quixote dreaming has bowed to Sancho Panza reality. Map courtesy Santa Barbara Trust for Historic Preservation

This rendering shows what the restored Presidio will look like when approached from Santa Barbara Street. Photo by William Dewey

The Mission, Santa Barbara's most famous landmark, was founded on December 4, 1786. The structure in the photograph dates from 1820. The so-called Queen of the California Missions is the only one to have remained throughout its history in the hands of the Franciscan padres. Courtesy UCSB Department of Special Collections

The Mission towers were destroyed in the 1925 earthquake. The facade has been completely restored and reinforced. Courtesy Santa Barbara News-Press

This interior shot shows the Santa Barbara Mission without pews. During the Spanish and Mexican periods, Indians and soldiers would kneel on blankets. Courtesy Dr. J. Walter Collinge

Franciscan padres at the Mission in 1872. Courtesy UCSB Department of Special Collections

Mission water systems usually involved using dams and aqueducts. The Mission dam in the Botanic Garden survives almost intact. Courtesy Santa Barbara Trust for Historic Preservation

Mission La Purisima was founded in 1787. The first mission built in the present-day town of Lompoc was utterly destroyed by the earthquake in 1812, causing the padres to relocate to a new site. By the end of the nineteenth century the mission buildings at the new site also had fallen into ruin. Courtesy UCSB Department of Special Collections

In the 1930s, La Purisima was restored and rebuilt as a WPA project. The Civilian Conservation Corps provided most of the physical labor. Architects, historians, and archaeologists lent their expertise to ensure historical authenticity. Courtesy UCSB Department of Special Collections

Tile making was done entirely by hand. Courtesy UCSB Department of Special Collections

Today La Purisima is a State Historic Park. It is considered one of the finest restorations in America. Courtesy Santa Barbara News-Press

This view of the original sanctuary at Mission Santa Ines, which was founded in 1804, typifies the richly decorated interiors found in the California missions. Mission Santa Ines, near Danish Solvang, was the site of the violent 1824 Chumash revolt that spread to Mission La Purisima and Santa Barbara. Courtesy Santa Barbara Trust for Historic Preservation

As the Presidio went into decline, soldiers and settlers built adobes outside the defense walls. One of the earliest was the Pico Adobe, which survives today and is part of the Presidio State Park. The precise date of its construction is not known. Courtesy Santa Barbara News-Press

Casa de la Guerra was built in the 1820s for Presidio comandante *Jose de la Guerra y Noriega. This 4,500-square-foot adobe mansion was visited by Richard Henry Dana and other well-known historical personages. It is owned by the Santa Barbara Trust for Historic Preservation and will be opened as a museum in 1989. Courtesy Santa Barbara Historical Society*

The interior of Casa de la Guerra as it appeared in the nineteenth century. Courtesy Santa Barbara Historical Society

Taken more than fifty years ago, this photo shows De la Guerra descendants on the veranda of the family mansion. Courtesy Santa Barbara Trust for Historic Preservation

Presidio descendants, left to right, Leroy Villa, Miguel Acosta, and Margarita Villa prepare a meal for a Trust for Historic Preservation event. They are members of "Los Descendientes," an organization founded recently for descendants of the Santa Barbara Presidio. Photo by Len Wood; Courtesy Santa Barbara News Press

The "Spirit of 1782" takes many forms. Though the costumes and type of dance seen in this photo at El Paseo are romanticized versions of early Santa Barbara's history, they reflect Santa Barbara's intense fascination with its Spanish heritage. Courtesy Santa Barbara Trust for Historic Preservation

Sentaro (1873-1939) and Tama (1882-1966) Asakura are shown with their children in a photograph taken before 1920. The Asakuras owned and ran a boarding house in the one hundred block of East Canon Perdido Street and also owned property in Japan. Two of their daughters are still alive, and numerous grandchildren and great-grandchildren live in Santa Barbara or elsewhere in California. Courtesy John and Julie (Asakura) Slagle

Chapter Three

Santa Barbara's Ethnic Heritage

The nineteenth century German philosopher Feuerbach's famous dictum: "Man is what he eats," plumbs the depths of the average Santa Barbaran's knowledge of his town's ethnic heritage. A visit to Oak Park on any given Sunday often provides the opportunity to nibble the food and enjoy the music and dance of the particular ethnic group that happens to be putting on a festival that day. Santa Barbara's ethnicity deserves more attention than this. It has played a significant role in the lives of scores of people in the community throughout Santa Barbara's history.

In terms of sheer numbers, the Chicano community is the most significant ethnic group. At least one third of the city of Santa Barbara's citizens are of Mexican origin. It is a community that has grown steadily since the turn of the century and is described in historical and scholarly accounts as being one of the oldest in the state. It once centered around the Old Presidio, but its locus today is the lower east side. Chicano cultural life, most visible during Cinco de Mayo, also includes religious celebrations such as the Feast Day of Our Lady of Guadalupe. Representing a synthesis of the Christian and Indian religious traditions, Our Lady of Guadalupe is the most powerful and complex cultural symbol of the Mexican heritage.

Although its presence has waned in recent years, Asian ethnicity was once a prominent part of Santa Barbara's cultural landscape. With the bleak exception of the internment of the Japanese during World War II, Santa Barbara has escaped racially provoked incidents such as took place against Chinese in San Francisco and Los Angeles. Santa Barbara once had a vibrant Chinatown located in the first block of East Canon Perdido Street. It was vividly described in Stewart Edward White's novel, *The Rose Dawn* (1920), as "a collection of battered old frame and adobe buildings that mysteriously had been lifted sheer from squalor to splendid romance by no other means than red paper, varnished ducks, rattan baskets, calico partitions, exotic smells and a brooding, spiritual atmosphere of the orient."

Just down the street in the next block between Anacapa and Santa Barbara Streets, the Japanese took up residence. There they stayed from 1900 until the World War II internment, eventually dispersing throughout the community after the war.

All told, a smaller amount of foreign immigrants settled in Santa Barbara than in large urban areas such as New York, Chicago, and San Francisco. As a result, with the exception of the Chicano and Asian groups, large ethnic enclaves and neighborhoods did not develop in this region as they did elsewhere.

Throughout its history, Santa Barbara has been influenced by three main cultural forces: the Euro-American coming from the East Coast or directly from Europe, the Latino moving up from the south, and the Asian from across the Pacific. It would be safe to say the Euro-American has been the dominant force since the nineteenth century, but that the Latino influence is going to be in the ascendant in the future. Whether this will lead to irreconcilable cultural conflict will depend on a community-wide awareness of and appreciation for Santa Barbara's ethnic heritage and a sympathetic attitude toward cultural pluralism.

The Chicano population of Santa Barbara represents our community's largest minority. Waves of migrations have continued to arrive in Santa Barbara since the end of the nineteenth century. California's first barrio emerged in the Presidio area and then later also developed on the lower east side. In this 1930s photograph a Chicana is being recognized for being "a good citizen and homemaker." Courtesy UCSB Department of Special Collections

During Christmas 1984 "La Pastorela" (The Shepherd's Play) was performed in the Santa Barbara Presidio Chapel, then under construction. An ancient tradition with roots in Mexico and Europe, the play is now performed annually in the Chapel by the Santa Barbara Latino community. The Santa Barbara version of the play is based on a script transcribed by Pablo de la Guerra in the nineteenth century. Photo by William Dewey

The Cortez sisters, Sylvia and Irma, and Alejandro Fernandez played the lead roles in "Una Pastorela" in 1986 and 1987. In the play the devils tempt the shepherds with the Seven Deadly Sins. But thanks to the intercession of San Miguel, the shepherds are saved and are able to present their gifts to Jesus in the manger. The play, adapted and put to music by Francisco Gonzalez, has brought the Chicano community back to the center of the city. Photo by William Dewey

Armando Vallejo, director of Casa de la Raza, with his two sons. The Casa, founded in the 1970s, is the cultural and social center of the Chicano community. Courtesy Casa de la Raza

El Teatro de la Esperanza, a Santa Barbara Chicano theatre group founded in the 1970s, is shown in rehearsal. The group moved to San Francisco in 1986. Courtesy Casa de la Raza

An example of Chicano mural art on Quarantina Street. Photo by William Dewey

The funeral of Miyoko Goto, age 13, on October 1, 1932, brought out nearly the entire Japanese community. This photograph was taken in front of the Japanese Buddhist Church, which was built in 1923, at 131 East Canon Perdido Street. Courtesy Hiro Goto

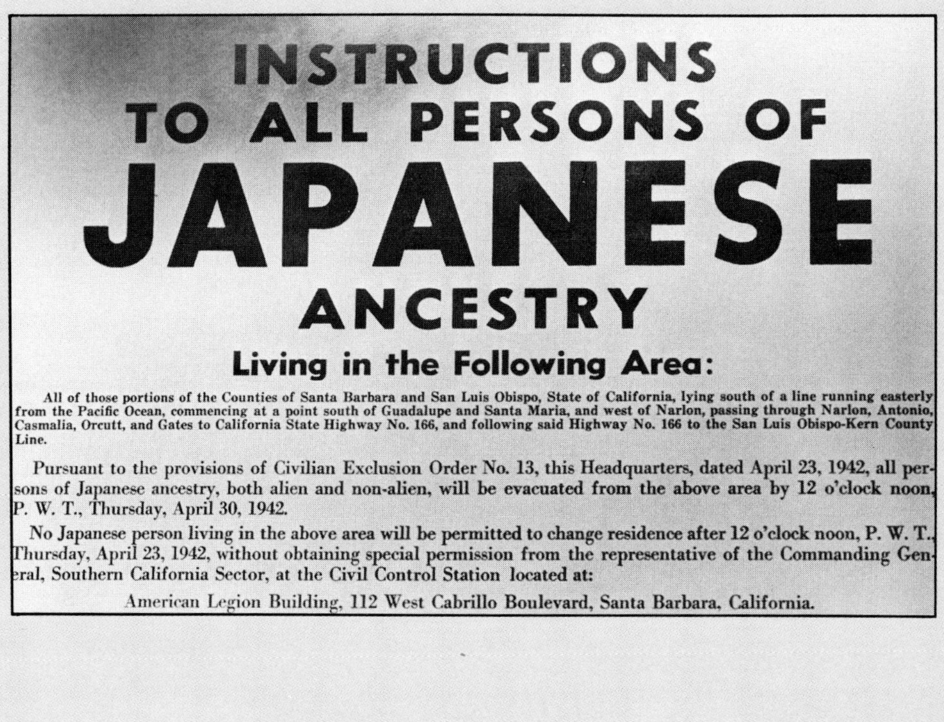

INSTRUCTIONS
TO ALL PERSONS OF
JAPANESE
ANCESTRY

Living in the Following Area:

All of those portions of the Counties of Santa Barbara and San Luis Obispo, State of California, lying south of a line running easterly from the Pacific Ocean, commencing at a point south of Guadalupe and Santa Maria, and west of Narlon, passing through Narlon, Antonio, Casmalia, Orcutt, and Gates to California State Highway No. 166, and following said Highway No. 166 to the San Luis Obispo-Kern County Line.

Pursuant to the provisions of Civilian Exclusion Order No. 13, this Headquarters, dated April 23, 1942, all persons of Japanese ancestry, both alien and non-alien, will be evacuated from the above area by 12 o'clock noon, P. W. T., Thursday, April 30, 1942.

No Japanese person living in the above area will be permitted to change residence after 12 o'clock noon, P. W. T., Thursday, April 23, 1942, without obtaining special permission from the representative of the Commanding General, Southern California Sector, at the Civil Control Station located at:

American Legion Building, 112 West Cabrillo Boulevard, Santa Barbara, California.

After the Japanese shelling of the Ellwood oil field in 1942, Santa Barbara Japanese received their "marching orders." For the duration of World War II, they were interned in a camp in Arizona on the Gila River. It was not one of Santa Barbara's proudest moments. Courtesy Santa Barbara News-Press

Most Italian immigrants began appearing in Santa Barbara in the early 1900s. The early wave brought the Raffettos, Mirattis, Pomattos, Cavalettos, Reginattos, Jordanos, Petrinis, and Castagnolas. These are all prominent names in Santa Barbara today. The Italians became restaurant operators and ranchers among other professions. There were also Italian stonemasons (about a hundred according to one estimate) mostly from the Veneto region, who did stonework in Montecito and on Alameda Padre Serra. Antolini, Dall'Armi, Bazzi, Goggia, Serena, and DaRos were among the best known stonemasons. Joe Buzzella (standing in the photo) was one of the Italian stonemasons who worked on the Mission restoration. Photo by Steve Malone; Courtesy Santa Barbara News-Press

Fugazi Bank opened up on State Street in 1913. Most of the Italian immigrants banked with Fugazi, finding it an easy way to send money to relatives back home. Courtesy Santa Barbara Historical Society

Francesco Franceschi (1843-1924) was one of Santa Barbara's most illustrious adopted citizens. He came from Florence where his family had suffered financial reverses, changed his name from Fenzi to Franceschi, and proceeded to pursue his passion for horticulture on his property on the Riviera. He was responsible for introducing a number of exotic plants to Santa Barbara, some of which still are growing on the Riviera hillside. Financial problems plagued him here as well and eventually he left for Tripoli in Africa in the service of the Italian government, dying there in 1924. His house and the surrounding garden are owned by the city of Santa Barbara. Photos courtesy Santa Barbara News-Press

One of Santa Barbara's leading citizens of Italian ancestry, George Castagnola (1908-1986), displayed a rare handsaw fish in 1950. His parents had come from Italy to Santa Barbara at the turn of the century. Courtesy Santa Barbara News-Press

Hans Sorensen and Bob Becker (two Danes in a dinghy?) participated in "Danish Days" celebration in 1968. A small but industrious Danish colony, arriving around 1910, founded Solvang, a small town that has become a major North County tourist attraction. Courtesy Santa Barbara News-Press

This windmill is a popular feature in Solvang.
Courtesy Santa Barbara News-Press

Santa Barbara's most famous Irishman lived in this house appropriately named "Hope House" after Thomas Hope, the man who built it in 1875. Hope, born in 1820 in Meath, Ireland, acquired the land that today is Hope Ranch and with the assistance of Chumash Indians and his majordomo Juan Justo, raised sheep on the acreage. Known for his fiery temper, he died of unknown causes in 1877. Vivian Obern, who owns the house, is seen giving a tour in 1965. Another nineteenth-century Irishman, Jack Powers, was one of Santa Barbara's most notorious citizens, eventually leaving town one step ahead of the law. In the twentieth century, Irishman Patrick Maher was Santa Barbara's mayor from 1937 to 1946. Courtesy Santa Barbara News-Press

This plaque is in the floor of the Presidio chapel. Photo by William Dewey

Robert Herdman, past president of the Santa Barbara Trust for Historic Preservation with Pete Tenoso and Ray Velasco of the Santa Barbara Filipino Community Association in 1983. Mr. Tenoso came to Santa Barbara from the Philippines in the 1920s and co-founded the Filipino Community Association in 1950. He was president, on and off, for sixteen years. Ray Velasco also arrived in Santa Barbara in the 1920s. According to a recent News-Press *article, there are today three thousand Filipinos in Santa Barbara. Courtesy Santa Barbara Trust for Historic Preservation*

On June 7, 1988, Filipina Gloria Megino Ochoa (left), shown celebrating with Chicana Raquel Mendoza, was elected first district supervisor of Santa Barbara County. Courtesy Christopher Gardner; Santa Barbara Independent

Today's Greek community of four hundred persons grew from a nucleus of six families who arrived here independently in the late 1930s, according to Dr. Ernest Kolendrianos, a Santa Barbara physician. In 1947 the Santa Barbara Greek Orthodox church was founded, and this photograph shows the ordination of Constantine Mitsopoulos, with Archbishop Athenagoras standing in the center. The church remains the focal point of the Greek community, and the annual Greek Festival the event where Greeks share their heritage with the community at large. Courtesy Santa Barbara Greek Orthodox Church

These Greek women attended an Easter picnic in Santa Barbara during the 1930s. Courtesy Santa Barbara Greek Orthodox Church

This magnificent Greek Orthodox Church was dedicated in 1986. In order to obtain a permit for its construction, the Greek community had to agree to a county-imposed curfew and other restrictions. This is yet another embarrassing moment in Santa Barbara's ethnic history. Photo by William Dewey

A fact not well known is that there were blacks among the soldiers at the Old Presidio in the eighteenth century. By 1887, a local newspaper reported the "colored colony" of Santa Barbara was increasing: "A year ago there were but two or three Negro families in town, while now they've become a familiar sight at every turn." According to an Afro-American Community History Project at UCSB, the major wave of black immigration here took place in the 1920s. In this 1926 photograph, blacks gathered in front of a house in Santa Barbara. One of Santa Barbara's leading citizens of the twentieth century, Pearl Chase, is standing in the back row, third from the right. Courtesy UCSB Department of Special Collections

Among Santa Barbara's most visible blacks has been Sam "Bam" Cunningham, graduate of Santa Barbara High, who went on to an All-American and professional career in football. Courtesy Santa Barbara News-Press

Hmong Chinese refugees from the Vietnam War settled for a while in Isla Vista, but most have been forced to move to the North Country because of local high rents. A fascinating people, they could be seen fishing evenings and weekends at the Goleta pier. Courtesy Santa Barbara News-Press

The Arlington House, which stood on the site of the present-day Safeway store at Chapala and Victoria streets, burned down in 1909. With ninety luxurious rooms, the hotel counted among its guests presidents Benjamin Harrison, William McKinley, and Theodore Roosevelt. Wrote one Santa Barbara historian: "After the climate, the Arlington has done more than any other agency toward giving Santa Barbara its favorable reputation as a health resort." Courtesy Santa Barbara Historical Society

Chapter Four

Elite in Eden

"We came not to conquer but to escape," might well be the motto of the waves of elite who have rolled up on the Santa Barbara shore. It was the Arlington House in the nineteenth century and the Potter Hotel in the twentieth that attracted the rich in the winter. Many became so entranced with the place that year after year more and more estates began to appear in Montecito.

The early elite came here to spend their fortunes, not to make them. It could have been otherwise. Take, for example, Dwight Murphy, a multimillionaire railroad magnate who at the age of forty-one retired in Santa Barbara in 1925. What if Murphy, instead of devoting himself to various civic causes and charities, had set his sights on promoting a real estate boom, tourism, or railroad expansion? There was a considerable amount of self-interest in his desire to preserve Santa Barbara from the jaws of industrialism. He already had his money and was looking for a place to enjoy the fruits of his labor and inheritance. What would have happened to Santa Barbara, to cite another cogent example, if Harrison Gray Otis, who spent four years in Santa Barbara in the nineteenth century, had stayed on and tried to build here the empire that made him one of the richest and most powerful men in Los Angeles? Instead, we got the more benign and benevolent owner and publisher of the *News-Press*, Tom Storke.

In one recent instance, actor Fess Parker, a member of the Santa Barbara elite, raised the hackles of a number of local citizens who believed he was bringing the town to the brink of overdevelopment. In the late 1970s Parker created a furor with his initial proposal for a hotel at the beach. After much hullabaloo, the project was scaled down, but it took a special initiative ballot vote before Parker was given the go-ahead to begin construction. The hotel finally opened in 1987.

Today the Santa Barbara elite is a different breed from the wealthy easterners who built Montecito mansions in the 1910s and 1920s. Now the wealthy come from various places, including foreign countries, and among them is a higher percentage of the Hollywood crowd—singers, actors, and other entertainment people. With a few exceptions they have not become as actively involved in the community. They are mostly "seclusion seekers."

Presidents, queens, princes, and a host of other celebrities have descended on Santa Barbara to partake of the sensual delights of the south-facing beaches surrounded by an amphitheater of purple mountains. It has been a "must stop" for visitors to the West Coast, and Santa Barbarans have gladly rolled out the red carpet, especially for royal visits.

But above all it is the "essential elite," those who have given their time and money to the community—the Fleischmanns, Murphys, Billingses, Peabodys, Grays, Knapps, and the like—who really matter. Whether the same kind of generous philanthropy will flow from the current crop of wealthy will depend on whether they feel their self-interest is intertwined with that of the common folk who also live here.

In 1902 the Potter Hotel was built at a cost of $1.5 million on the beach at Santa Barbara. The luxury hotel could accommodate up to one thousand guests and had a grand dining room with a capacity of six hundred for banquets. The opening of the hotel brought hundreds of wealthy easterners who wintered in Santa Barbara. A number of them, impressed with Santa Barbara's natural beauty and equable climate, began building enormous mansions in Montecito. Thus began the parade of elite that has been descending on Santa Barbara ever since. The hotel was destroyed by fire in 1923. Photos courtesy Santa Barbara Historical Society

William H. Bliss, a highly respected St. Louis attorney, stands before his Montecito mansion. He first came to Santa Barbara shortly before World War I with his wealthy New York socialite wife and together they developed the rambling Casa Dorinda estate. Bliss's wife, Anna Dorinda, gave money to the Botanic Garden and Cottage Hospital, a philanthropy typical of a number of the rich who took up residence in Montecito. Courtesy Santa Barbara News-Press

Casa Dorinda, the Bliss mansion designed by the prominent architect Carleton Winslow, was the scene of frequent lavish parties, receptions for royalty such as King Albert and Queen Elizabeth of Belgium, and concerts by notables such as Jascha Heifetz. It has been converted into an upscale retirement community. Courtesy Santa Barbara News-Press

Dwight Murphy (1892-1976) was the son of a wealthy railroad magnate who was one of the Easterners attracted to Santa Barbara by the Potter Hotel. After spending three years of his youth here, he returned to Pittsburgh where he eventually became president of his father's railroad company. Retiring at forty-one in 1925, Murphy took up permanent residence in Santa Barbara. Known for his successful breeding of palominos, Murphy was also a tireless worker in support of various civic causes, served on the parks and planning commissions, and donated to numerous charities. Courtesy Santa Barbara News-Press

Max Fleischmann, the so-called "yeast king" and one of the richest men in the world, lived on his estate, Edgewood, on Lambert Road in Summerland from 1921 to 1956. His local benefactions included funding for the Museum of Natural History, the harbor breakwater, St. Vincent's School, and Cottage Hospital. He also established the Santa Barbara Foundation. At seventy-four he developed inoperable pancreatic cancer and committed suicide. Courtesy Santa Barbara Historical Society

The trophy room in Fleischmann's mansion testifies to the success of his many big game hunts. The trophies are now on permanent display in the Fleischmann Memorial Room and Library at the Museum of Natural History. Courtesy Santa Barbara Historical Society

Fleischmann's yacht, Haida, *was moored in the harbor. Courtesy Santa Barbara* News-Press

A 1909 graduate of the University of Illinois in civil engineering, Avery Brundage made millions in the 1920s as a Chicago contractor, a fortune he lost in the depression but recouped in later years in real estate investments. He is best remembered as the president of the International Olympic Committee. In this 1957 photograph he is shown with his wife in front of their Santa Barbara mansion. In the 1950s he owned both El Paseo and the Montecito Country Club. His mansion, containing priceless art objects, was destroyed by the 1964 Coyote Canyon fire. He died in 1975. Courtesy Santa Barbara News-Press

Ganna Walska, a Polish beauty who lived in the famous Montecito estate called Lotusland, had the uncanny knack for marrying millionaires. Born in obscurity in Poland in 1883, she went to Russia in her youth, where she married a wealthy baron and became a member of high society, including the czar's social set. She was married six times to husbands whose combined wealth was well over $100 million. She took up residence in Santa Barbara around 1940 and is seen in a 1958 photograph with Dr. Kurt von Schuschnigg, second from left, the Austrian political leader forced out of power during the Nazi period, and Baron and Baroness Torrosani. Courtesy Santa Barbara News-Press

Lotusland, operated by a foundation set up by Ganna Walska, will soon be open for limited public tours. Courtesy Santa Barbara News-Press

Among the elite who have visited Santa Barbara has been a parade of United States presidents. President McKinley, second from left, is shown with members of his cabinet touring the Santa Barbara Mission garden in 1900. In the nineteenth century, Rutherford B. Hayes and Benjamin Harrison were two other presidents who paid visits to Santa Barbara. Courtesy Santa Barbara Historical Society

President Teddy Roosevelt gave a speech at the beach in Santa Barbara in 1903. He is shown in the lower left center leaning assertively toward the audience in a typical TR pose. Courtesy Santa Barbara Historical Society

Presidential candidate Herbert Hoover visited Santa Barbara on the campaign trail in 1928. The handsome Hoover posed for a photo in the Street in Spain at El Paseo. The gentleman standing at the far right is Bernhard Hoffmann, the developer who built El Paseo. Hoover won the presidential election easily, but the Great Depression was just around the corner. Courtesy Santa Barbara Trust for Historic Preservation

Governor Earl Warren, later Chief Justice of the Supreme Court, and then-United States Senator Richard Nixon enjoyed a Fiesta parade with their families in 1952. A close friend of News-Press *editor Tom Storke, Warren was a frequent visitor to Santa Barbara. Actor Leo Carrillo, wearing white hat, is apparently signing an autograph book. Courtesy Santa Barbara Historical Society*

John Fitzgerald Kennedy and his new bride, Jacqueline, strolled along the paths of San Ysidro Ranch during their honeymoon in Santa Barbara in 1953, an early glimpse of this Camelot couple whose life together came to an abrupt end on a Dallas street in 1963. Courtesy Hal Boucher

Robert Kennedy and his wife, Ethel, were photographed on their honeymoon in Santa Barbara in the 1950s. Courtesy Santa Barbara News-Press

Robert Kennedy returned to Santa Barbara on the presidential campaign trail in 1968, giving a speech on May 29 at UCSB. A few days later, his life came to a tragic end after a victory speech in Los Angeles's Ambassador Hotel, when, like his brother, he was killed by an assassin's bullet. Coming two months after Martin Luther King's murder, Kennedy's death made 1968 one of the bleakest years in American history. Courtesy Santa Barbara News-Press

Ronald Reagan and wife Nancy were all smiles at their ranch in 1981. The photo was taken just a few days before he took the presidential oath of office. The popular president and first lady have not visited downtown Santa Barbara during his presidency, but in 1970, while governor of California, he gave a speech at El Paseo during the student upheaval at UCSB. His speech triggered a riot that resulted in angry students breaking windows on State Street. Courtesy Santa Barbara News-Press

The Reagan Ranch is nestled in the hillside above the old Ortega Rancho, which dates from Spanish times. Photo by Steve Malone; Courtesy Santa Barbara News-Press

The most remarkable fact about President Reagan's ranch is its unpretentiousness. During his two terms in office, the President has made frequent visits to the Western White House. Photo by Bob Ponce; Courtesy Santa Barbara News-Press

Soviet Premier Nikita S. Khrushchev stopped off in Santa Barbara on September 29, 1959, during his tour of the United States. Mayor Paulson of Los Angeles had insulted him, Khrushchev said, but he received a warm welcome from Santa Barbara Mayor Edward A. Abbott. After but a short visit, the Russian climbed back on the train and sped away. Courtesy Santa Barbara News-Press

Over the years Santa Barbara has rolled out the red carpet for royalty from England, Spain, and other countries. One of the most celebrated visits was that of Queen Elizabeth II of England in 1983. She came during one of the fiercest winters Santa Barbara has ever experienced, but, undaunted, she climbed the stairs of the Mission with Father Virgil Cordano. Photo by Rafael Maldonado; Courtesy Santa Barbara News-Press

Actor Ronald Colman with his wife and daughter in Santa Barbara in 1949. The actor was among the Hollywood stars attracted to the area. He became co-owner of the San Ysidro Ranch in the 1940s. Among the most visible actors who spent time in Santa Barbara prior to World War II were Leo Carrillo and Rita Hayworth, both of whom frequented the El Paseo Restaurant. Courtesy Santa Barbara News-Press

Montecito resident, comedian Jonathan Winters, makes public appearances on behalf of local charities. He recently published a book entitled Winters' Tales *that has made it to the best seller list. Photo by Lesley Newhart; Courtesy Santa Barbara* News-Press

Another celebrity who has become active in the community is singer Kenny Loggins (right) with his wife and Senator Alan Cranston. In 1987, Loggins donated his talents to a children's Christmas fund-raiser. Courtesy Santa Barbara News-Press

Actress Eva Marie Saint has been a Santa Barbara resident for a number of years. Photo by Len Wood; Courtesy Santa Barbara News-Press

For the generation that grew up in the 1950s, Santa Barbara resident Fess Parker will always be Davy Crockett, King of the Wild Frontier. Courtesy Walt Disney Productions

For Santa Barbarans, Fess Parker will be best remembered as the man who built the Red Lion Inn Resort. Photo by Len Wood; Courtesy Santa Barbara News-Press

In 1982, then-Chancellor Robert Huttenback presented an award to UCSB graduate Michael Douglas. The actor premiered his movie "Romancing the Stone" in Santa Barbara as a fund-raiser for the university. He won best actor at the 1988 Academy Awards for his performance as Gordon Gekko in the movie Wall Street. *Photo by Len Wood; Courtesy Santa Barbara* News-Press

A little girl was photographed in her Fiesta costume in 1928. Courtesy UCSB Department of Special Collections

Chapter Five

Hometown Hoi Polloi

Americans love the rags-to-riches story—the notion that any hardworking, enterprising individual can climb to the top. For every one of those who have made it, there are thousands of others who have, as it were, stayed put. These are the common folk—the hoi polloi—who work, play, and fade away into the stream of history.

The hoi polloi of Santa Barbara, past and present, have participated in a whole gamut of daily and ordinary activities that until recently have slipped by the historian unnoticed. There is a kind of unself-consciousness among the hoi polloi, a sense of taking life as it is and extracting enjoyment from the simple and basic.

If the rich are the pillars of society, the hoi polloi are the backbone, people who have accepted their role in the scheme of things. But in the faces of the hoi polloi, one sees the uniqueness of each individual, the anger, the humor, the natural, the uncontrived. The hoi polloi are the essence of the democratic spirit.

Andy Warhol said that in the future everybody would be famous for fifteen minutes, an interesting thought that evokes images of people stepping forward before the camera for a few minutes so to speak, and then moving off stage, back into anonymity. The "snapshot" of the common folk freezes time in an unrehearsed moment; a snap of a second becomes eternity.

If the great fear of the high achiever and the nouveau riche is that they may backslide and be swallowed up by the great mass of humanity, they should fear not. The flotsam and the jetsam, the hoboes, the working stiff, the history teacher, the high school football player are all too busy with their own lives, with their own peccadilloes, foibles, and eccentricities, to swallow up anybody.

A simpler time is reflected in this photo of a group of Santa Barbarans on a chaperoned camping trip on Santa Cruz Island circa 1897. Courtesy Midge Hayes

A spot of tea being shared on Santa Cruz Island. Courtesy Midge Hayes

A couple on the camping trip enjoy the pleasure of each other's company. Courtesy Midge Hayes

The Santa Barbara High School Class of 1893 posed for this portrait. Courtesy Santa Barbara News-Press

Children are shown with teachers and a dog in front of a turn-of-the-century Summerland school house. Courtesy Santa Barbara News-Press

Domestic violence in Santa Barbara in the 1890s ended with the hanging of Ramon Lopez, convicted of murdering his wife. Photos courtesy Santa Barbara Historical Society

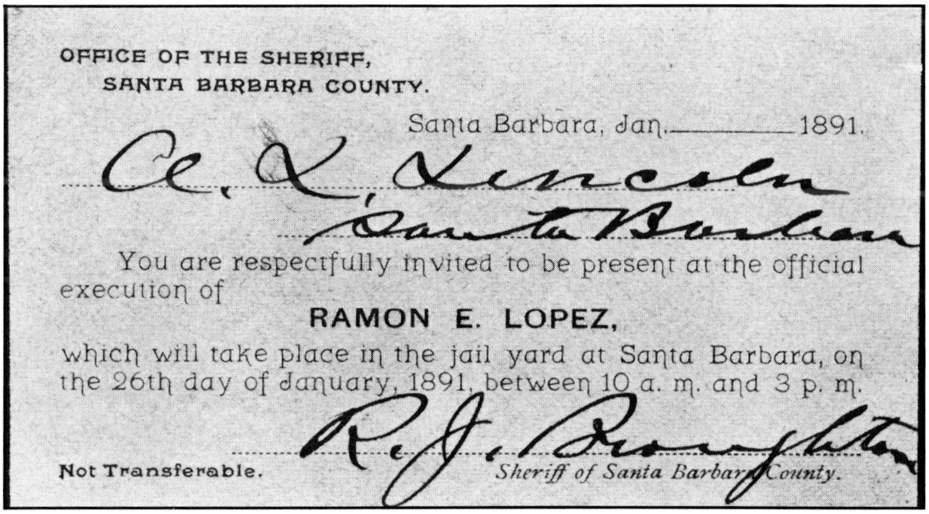

OFFICE OF THE SHERIFF,
SANTA BARBARA COUNTY.

Santa Barbara, Jan.________1891.

C. L. Lincoln
Santa Barbara

You are respectfully invited to be present at the official execution of

RAMON E. LOPEZ,

which will take place in the jail yard at Santa Barbara, on the 26th day of January, 1891, between 10 a. m. and 3 p. m.

R. J. Broughton
Sheriff of Santa Barbara County.

Not Transferable.

This Indian woman was photographed outside a Santa Barbara adobe. Courtesy UCSB Department of Special Collections

Martin Erro was photographed while working the land at the Orella Ranch, east of Refugio Canyon in the 1920s. Courtesy the Hvolboll Family

A sheep herder about his business on San Miguel Island in the 1940s. Courtesy Santa Barbara News Press

Uniformed Santa Barbara Girl Scouts posed in 1926. Courtesy UCSB Department of Special Collections

Santa Barbara students are shown learning how to brush their teeth in 1933. Courtesy UCSB Department of Special Collections

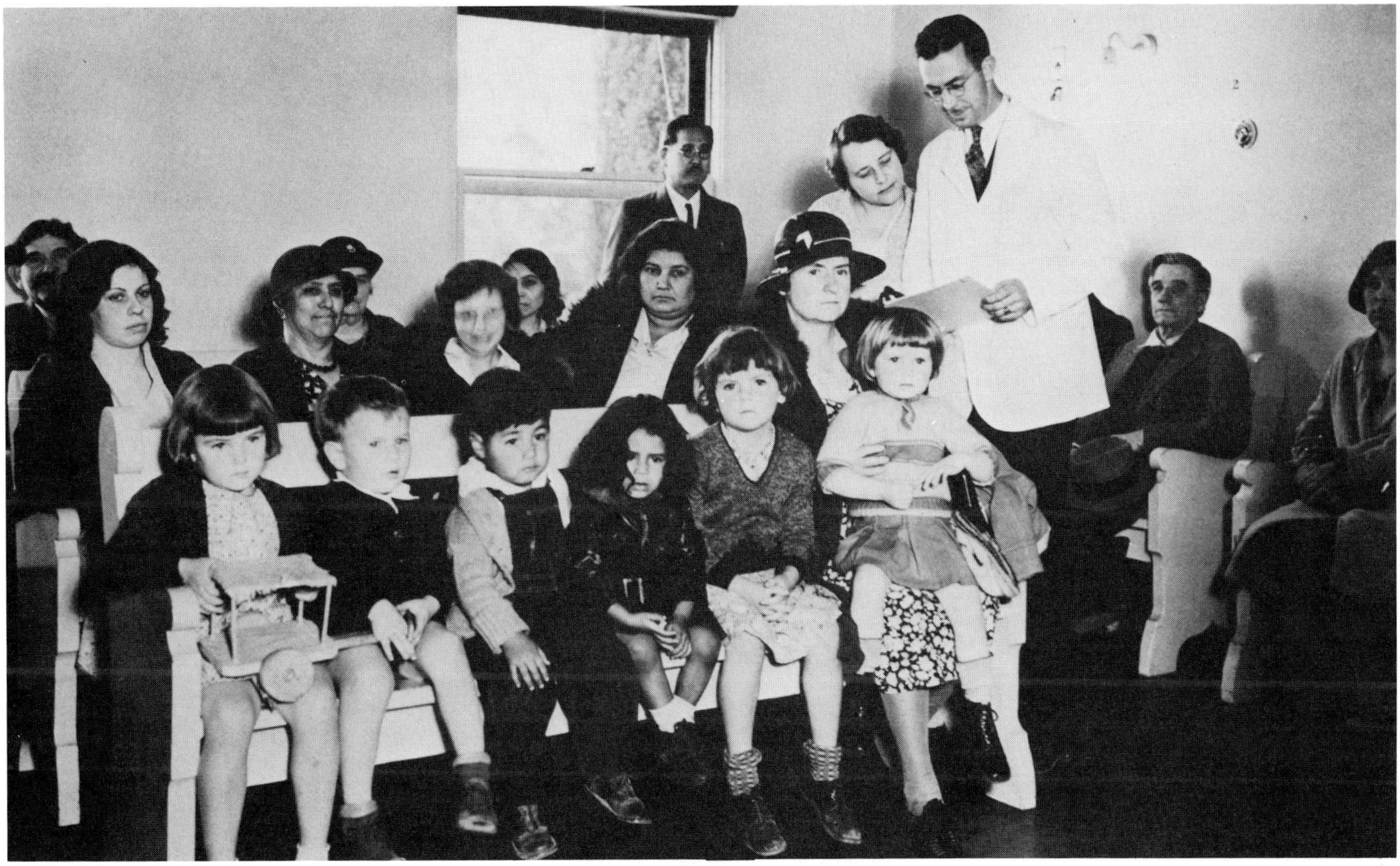

A 1933 Chamber of Commerce health contest brought Santa Barbara's hoi polloi to the Cottage Hospital Dispensary for check-ups. Courtesy UCSB Department of Special Collections

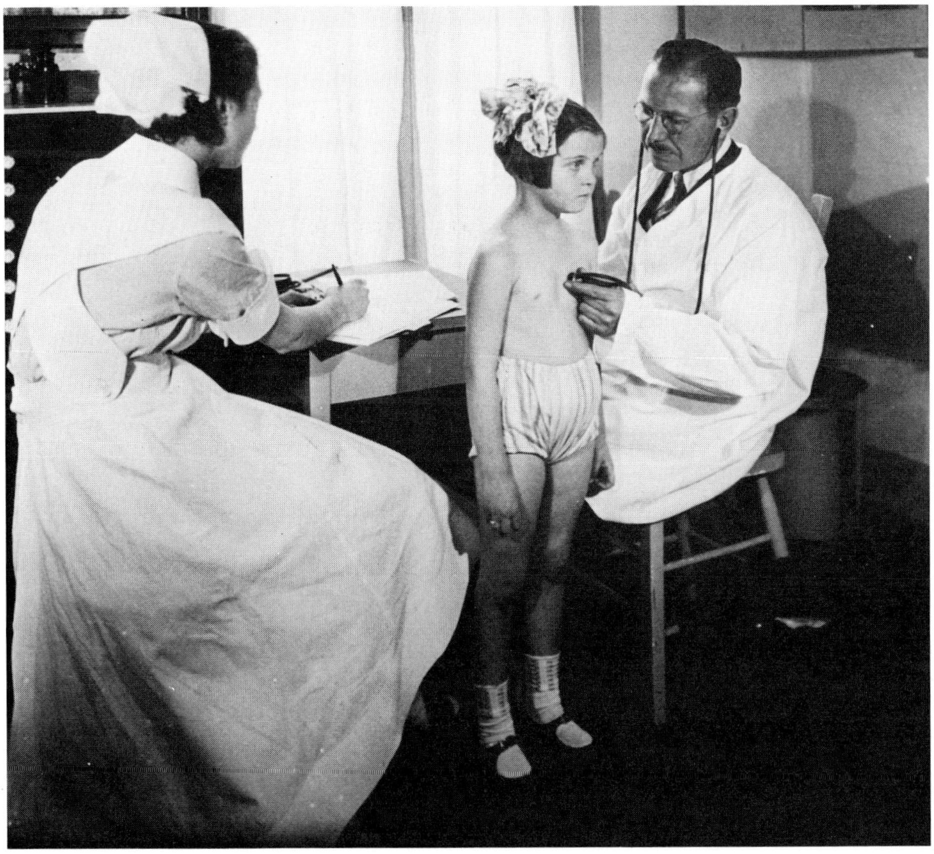

A young girl is examined at the Cottage Hospital Dispensary in the 1930s. Courtesy UCSB Department of Special Collections

Polio and the iron lung were the nightmares of parents and children in the post World War II generation—until the Salk vaccine saved the day. Here a patient is being treated at the County Hospital in 1948. Courtesy Santa Barbara News-Press

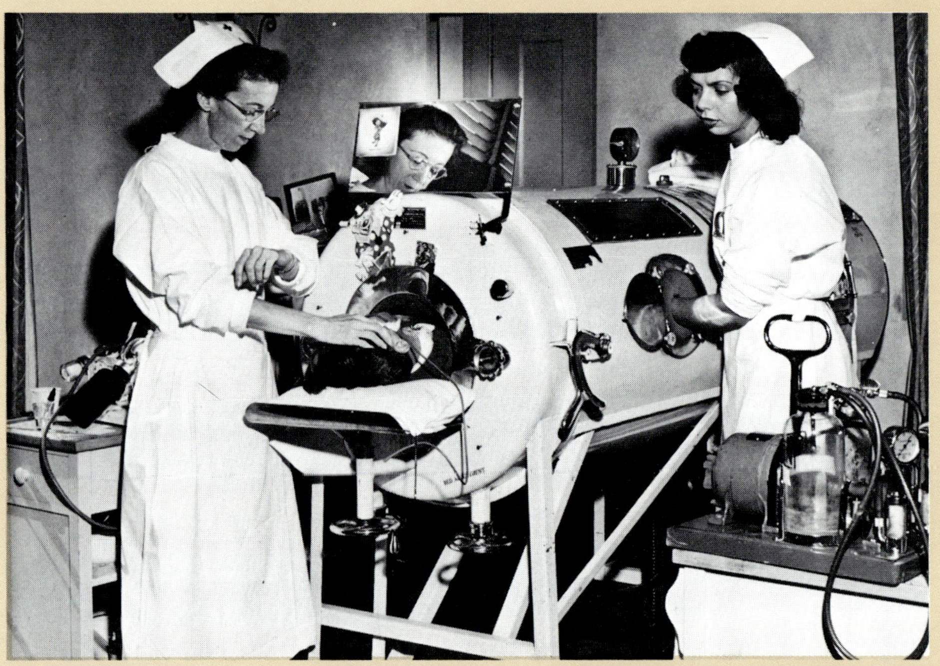

An unidentified photograph in the Pearl Chase Collection at UCSB is a Santa Barbara version of Edward Hopper's famous painting, Nighthawks. Courtesy UCSB Department of Special Collections

These young women were being serenaded at Restaurante El Paseo in the 1920s. Courtesy UCSB Department of Special Collections

A service station at Islay and State streets in the 1920s waits for business. Courtesy UCSB Department of Special Collections

Prices varied at this gas station at Anapamu and Chapala (date unknown). Courtesy Reyes Foxen

Filling up in Santa Barbara at 17½ cents per gallon. This was long before OPEC appeared on the scene. Courtesy UCSB Department of Special Collections

Santa Barbara High School baseball players posed for this photo in 1904. Courtesy Santa Barbara News-Press

Once in a while a member of the hoi polloi achieves fame. This photo is of Eddie Matthews, graduate of Santa Barbara High School in 1949, who went on to become the perennial all-star third baseman of the Milwaukee Braves. He's the only Santa Barbaran to have been inducted into Baseball's Hall of Fame. Courtesy Santa Barbara News-Press

You meet "a lot" of people on a Honda. These two Santa Barbara High football players are on their way to practice. Courtesy Santa Barbara News-Press

The fishing looks good at Stearns Wharf in 1956. Courtesy Santa Barbara News-Press

A latter day Huck Finn and Tom Sawyer were fishing at Stearns Wharf in 1961. Courtesy Santa Barbara News-Press

A Sunday crowd is shown gathered on Goleta Pier in 1984. Photo by Steve Malone; Courtesy Santa Barbara News-Press

The Hobo village at the Child's Estate as photographed in 1951. Courtesy Santa Barbara News-Press

Joe Troy is pictured drawing at Hobo Village in 1949. Photo courtesy Santa Barbara News-Press

Hoboes at the Child's Estate. Courtesy Santa Barbara News-Press

Santa Barbara's Loud family became celebrities when their private lives were laid bare on a public television documentary in 1972. The Louds' marriage broke up as a national television audience looked on. Courtesy Santa Barbara News-Press

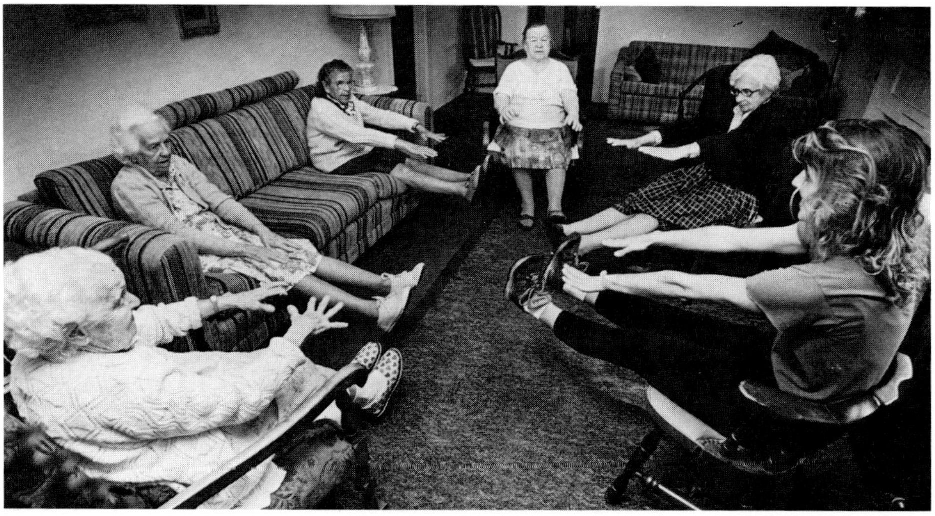

Residents of a Santa Barbara retirement home in 1986 are shown exercising. Photo by Len Wood; Courtesy Santa Barbara News-Press

A tree among the hoi polloi is the Moreton Bay Fig Tree. A designated city landmark, it dates from the nineteenth century. Courtesy UCSB Department of Special Collections

The cycle of life can be seen at Shoreline Park. Photos by Steve Malone and Bob Ponce; Courtesy Santa Barbara News-Press

Beautiful seascapes lull Santa Barbarans into thinking that mother nature is truly benevolent. But nature can rear its ugly head and turn earth, fire, water, and air into a demonic cauldron of chaos. Photo by Rafael Maldonado; Courtesy Santa Barbara News-Press

Chapter Six

Trouble in Paradise

Violent fits come crashing through the calm. The four elements break loose and the Santa Barbara paradise is suddenly in upheaval:

First, fire: scorching flames leaping across hillsides, smoke billowing, ashes falling like snow flakes.

Next, the wind: "Sparks and embers blowing down the canyons"; after the fire is gone, the wind kicks up again, swirling and smashing; trees are bent by the "Santannas."

Then, the rain: a soft sprinkle turns into a monstrous downpour—sheets of liquid coming out of the sky.

Even terra firma loses its grip: the good, old, reliable earth begins to shake and quake—sending people into the streets.

On clear, crisp days, the sculpted Santa Ynez Mountains and the azure ocean delight the eye. On cool, foggy spring days, a torpor prevails and the bones ache a little. All is well. But looming out there are catastrophe and disaster: the thirty-second shake, the two-hour downpour and the one-day conflagration, and 364 days of bliss are wiped away.

This doom and gloom scenario seems Wagnerian, more tortured imagination than reality. But those who have lived in Santa Barbara a while know that this fiction can become all too real. Intellectually, it is exciting (Faustian!) to think that something wicked can happen at any moment—it's part of living in Santa Barbara, a figment of fear stirring around in our collective unconscious. Step forward, Prospero and let us experience your magic powers.

The Coyote Fire in 1964 raged out of control in Mission Canyon above the Botanic Garden. Brush fires come in the summer and especially in the early fall when the hillsides turn to tinderboxes. Fires have been recurring calamities in Santa Barbara since Spanish times. In the 1830s one fire burned right down to the edge of the town terrorizing the citizenry who sought refuge in Don Jose de la Guerra's mansion. Courtesy Santa Barbara News-Press

This 1971 photograph shows the Romero Canyon Fire with the city in the foreground. Courtesy Santa Barbara News-Press

A change in wind direction spelled disaster for this truck during the Romero fire in 1971. Courtesy Santa Barbara News-Press

Most frightening of all is when fires burn toward homes as seen in this photo of the Romero fire. Courtesy Santa Barbara News-Press

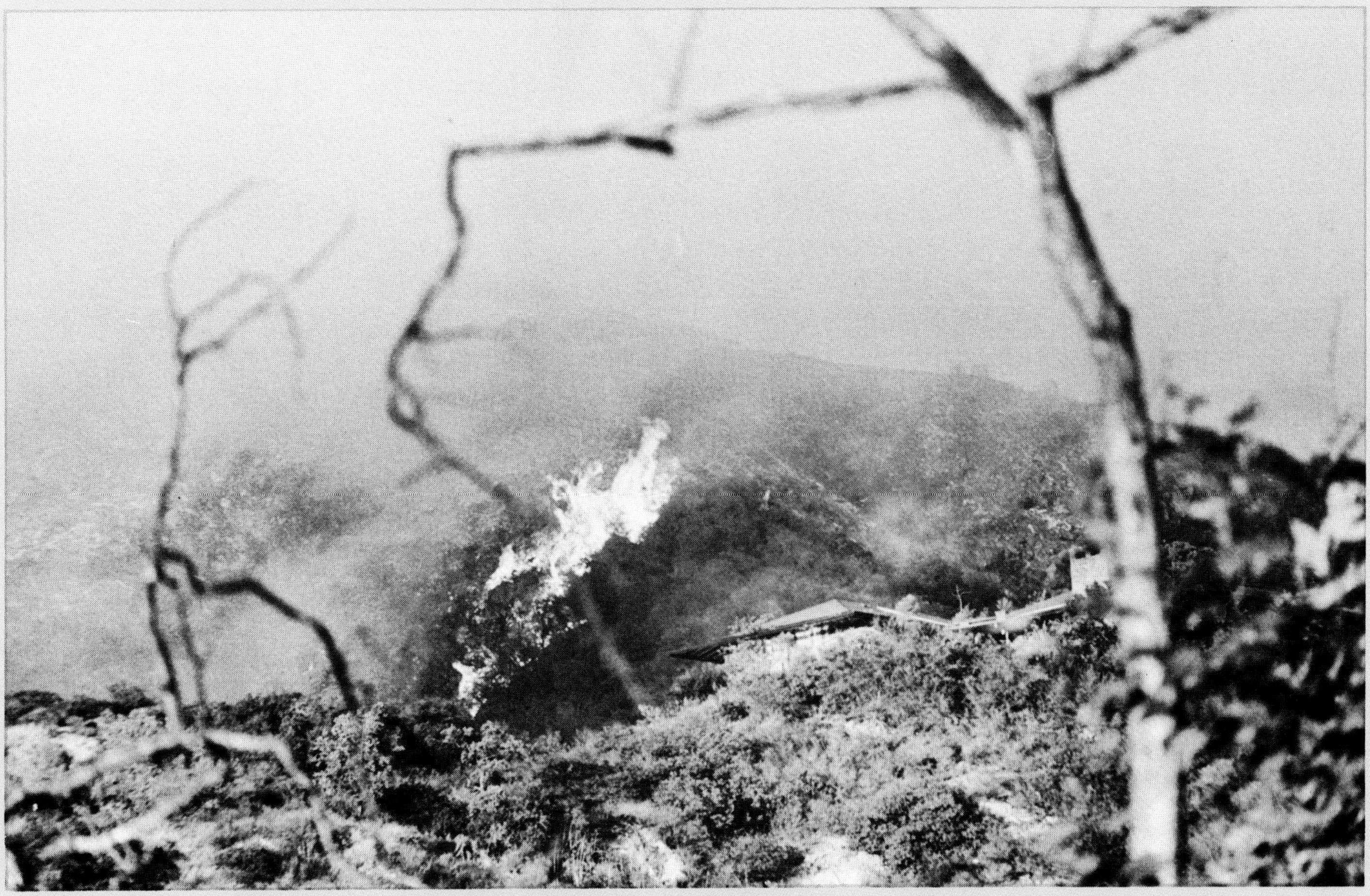

After the fire, a sign takes on a sardonic quality. Courtesy Santa Barbara News-Press

The 1977 Sycamore canyon fire with flames shooting hundreds of feet in the air, burned out of control toward Santa Barbara. Courtesy Santa Barbara News-Press

The serendipity of the 1977 fire is seen in this photo—one home completely razed, the other in the background unscathed. Photo by Bob Ponce; Courtesy Santa Barbara News-Press

Floods can be fun. In 1952, a Buick became a power boat plowing through water in the four hundred block of Alisos Street. Courtesy Santa Barbara News-Press

In 1967 the Santa Barbara airport became an island. When the so-called hundred year floods come, anything can happen. Courtesy Paul Harvey, United Airlines

The brute force of water raging down the mountainside is captured in this photo during a 1969 storm. Fifteen inches of rain fell in a twelve hour period, causing flooding of Old Testament proportions. Courtesy Santa Barbara News-Press

A Montecito home is washed away in the 1969 flood. Courtesy Santa Barbara *News-Press*

This lucky horse was saved from a quagmire following the 1969 flood. Courtesy Santa Barbara *News-Press*

Storms brewing offshore have a long history of wreaking havoc on ships and the coastline. Powerful winds called "southeasters" have been the most notorious. Richard Henry Dana vividly described a southeaster in his classic, Two Years Before the Mast. *This 1961 photo shows a boat ramming into Stearns Wharf. Courtesy Santa Barbara* News-Press

1983 was one of the worst storm years in recent memory. It was the year of "El Niño," a shift in ocean currents that resulted in storm after storm slamming into Santa Barbara. The recently restored Stearns Wharf was battered and bruised. Photo by Bob Ponce; Courtesy Santa Barbara News-Press

A ravaged Leadbetter Beach was inspected by the curious in 1983. Courtesy Santa Barbara News-Press

Palm Park looked like a war zone in 1983. Courtesy Santa Barbara News-Press

A wave pounds Rincon Beach in 1983. Damage to private property was heavy along the coast from Rincon to Miramar Beaches. Courtesy Santa Barbara News-Press

On June 29, 1925, a violent earthquake measuring 6.3 on the Richter scale struck Santa Barbara. The San Marcos Building on the corner of State and Victoria streets suffered severe damage. Of all the natural disasters, none is more frightening than the earthquake, which comes without warning. In 1806, 1812, and 1857 Santa Barbara experienced earthquakes of even greater magnitude than the 1925 temblor. A huge seismic wave came ashore in 1812. Courtesy Santa Barbara Historical Society

The Hotel Californian was finished four days before the 1925 earthquake. After $50,000 worth of repairs the building was finally re-opened; it is still a hotel today and the home of Rocky Galenti's Bar. Courtesy Santa Barbara Historical Society

Most of the furniture appears intact in the Hotel Californian. Courtesy UCSB Department of Special Collections

Inspectors and workmen gather to assess damage to the Hotel Californian. Courtesy Santa Barbara Historical Society

Our Lady of Sorrows Church, an adobe structure located at State and Figueroa, was a total loss. The church was the successor church of the Presidio chapel, which had been destroyed by the 1857 Fort Tejon earthquake. Courtesy Santa Barbara Historical Society

This family was left frightened and homeless by the 1925 earthquake. Courtesy Santa Barbara Historical Society

The building at the corner of State and de la Guerra streets was damaged and then demolished. Courtesy Santa Barbara Historical Society

The corner of State and de la Guerra ended up looking like this in 1926. Today it is the site of the Westen's Camera building. Courtesy UCSB Department of Special Collections

In 1925 the famous Mission towers came tumbling down. Courtesy Santa Barbara News-Press

In 1978 a brief but powerful jolt shook books from shelves in the UCSB Library. Courtesy Santa Barbara News-Press

One of the victims of the 1978 temblor was photographed during recovery. Photo by Rafael Maldonado; Courtesy Santa Barbara News-Press

A *drug store in Goleta had to face this mess after the 1978 earthquake. Courtesy Santa Barbara* News-Press

A reinforced concrete support was sheared off, forcing closure of the Ward Memorial Blvd. while the overpass was repaired. Photo by Bob ponce; courtesy Santa Barbara News-Press

The 1978 quake also caused a derailment. For the historical record: a 3.9 earthquake rocked Santa Barbara during the week the captions for this chapter were written. Photo by Steve Malone; Courtesy Santa Barbara News-Press

The Fox Arlington Theatre replaced the Arlington Hotel, which had been demolished after the 1925 earthquake. Courtesy Santa Barbara Trust for Historic Preservation

Chapter Seven

The Triumph of Hispanic Architecture

The American architect Louis Sullivan said: "The building without reflects the people within." A survey of Santa Barbara's architecture tells us very much indeed about the people who have lived here—about their backgrounds, their needs, their dreams.

Santa Barbara began as a mud fort, with adobe dwellings spreading helter-skelter around town until the 1850s. Then the Americans began to take over, and unleashed their compulsion to bring order to what they considered the Mexican chaos: they laid out a grid system, introduced fired-brick buildings, and later, Victorian frame houses; developed a "Main Street" and called it "State Street" and felt a smug satisfaction that all was better.

But the Mexican world did not die out entirely—some adobes survived into the twentieth century. After the 1925 earthquake, Santa Barbara's built environment changed directions again when a conscious decision was made to "de-Americanize" the town by rebuilding it in a Spanish/Mexican/Mediterranean style. New Englanders who had taken up residence in Santa Barbara formed a committee and decided to create a "New Spain."

This decision is a little less ironic than it appears at first blush. The Santa Barbara coastline faces south like that of southern Spain and the climate and play of light here give the region a natural Mediterranean flavor. Not surprisingly, the architect who designed El Paseo, James Osborne Craig, spent childhood summers in Andalusia. El Paseo, built in 1923, is quintessential Santa Barbara architecture with its white-washed walls and wrought iron windows and ornamentation. It served as the primary model for rebuilding the City after the earthquake of 1925.

To put it quite simply: its architectural unity is what has made Santa Barbara such a special place. The gifted architects of the 1920s and 1930s, Craig, Winslow, Smith, Edwards, Plunkett, and the like, are cultural heroes—as are those citizens who encouraged them—especially the indomitable Pearl Chase and Bernhard and Irene Hoffmann. They should be memorialized in statues in the fashion of the *Burghers of Calais*—and from their pedestals look out happily over their achievement.

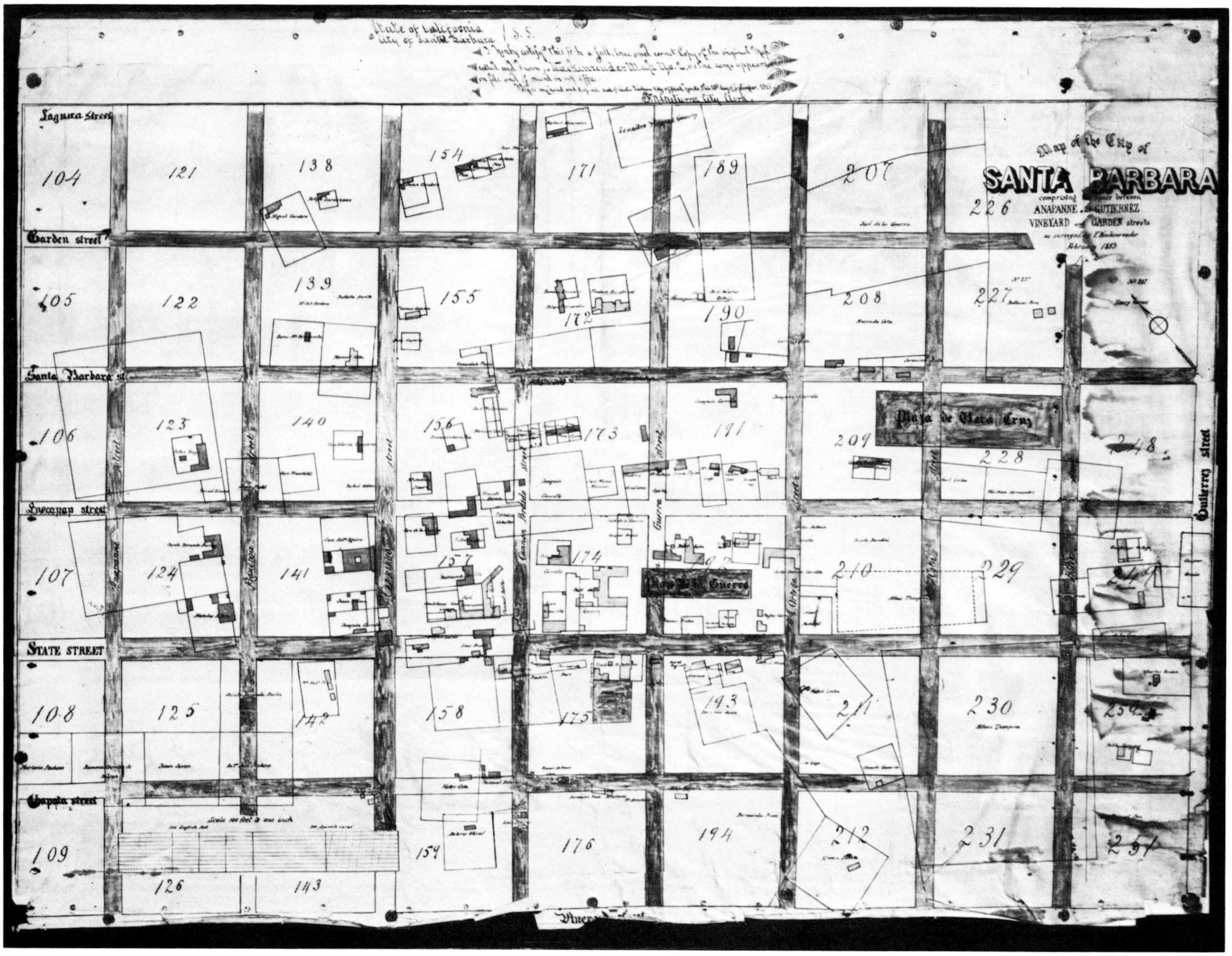

This 1853 map of Santa Barbara graphically illustrates the conflict between the Mexican and American ideas of towns. During the Spanish and Mexican periods the pueblo grew outward from the Presidio, with adobes appearing randomly around the fort. This was alien to Americans who laid out a standard grid system, leaving adobes right in the center of the streets. It took several decades before roadways were cleared. Courtesy Santa Barbara Trust for Historic Preservation

One historian wrote in the early twentieth century: "The old adobes were scorned as old fashioned. Adobes became the cheapest place in town to rent." This attitude led to the neglect of the adobes, and today only a handful of these treasures from the past survive. Courtesy Santa Barbara Historical Society

Alpheus Thompson (1797-1869) was one of the several dozen Americans who arrived during the Mexican period and married into an old California family. He built the famous Thompson Adobe. Courtesy Santa Barbara Trust for Historic Preservation

Alpheus Thompson's adobe as it was depicted by artist Alexander Harmer. Courtesy Santa Barbara Historical Society

The Thompson Adobe, seen at right in this photograph, has become the subject of a historical debate. Until recently, it was thought that the Larkin House in Monterey was the first two-story adobe built in California. Further research has uncovered that the Thompson Adobe was built in 1834 and thus predates the 1835 construction of the Larkin House. Courtesy Santa Barbara News-Press

Eventually the Thompson Adobe became the St. Charles Hotel, an early example of "adaptive re-use." The adobe, located on the site of the present-day Piccadilly Square, was torn down in 1913. Courtesy Santa Barbara Trust for Historic Preservation

With the arrival of the train in 1887, Santa Barbara was "on track" to becoming "Americanized." Courtesy Santa Barbara News-Press

Colonel W. W. Hollister (1818-1886), called "the foremost figure in the Americanization of Santa Barbara," drove five thousand sheep from the midwest to California, settling in Northern California. In 1867 he moved with his family to Santa Barbara. Besides developing a showcase farm around his Glen Annie house just west of present-day Goleta, Hollister financed construction of Stearns Wharf, the Lobero Theatre and the ninety-room Arlington House Hotel. Courtesy Santa Barbara Historical Society

What could be more American-looking than this State Street store front? Courtesy Santa Barbara Historical Society

Founded in the 1870s and 1880s, the Santa Barbara Daily News *and* Independent, *later to evolve into the* News-Press, *were two early newspapers reflecting the emerging Anglo influence. Courtesy Santa Barbara* News-Press

State Street at the corner of Canon Perdido Street as it appeared in 1908. Courtesy Santa Barbara News-Press

The Commercial Trust & Savings Bank located on State Street was built prior to the 1925 earthquake. Courtesy Santa Barbara Trust for Historic Preservation

This Victorian house at 821 Coronel was typical of turn-of-the century residences. Courtesy Santa Barbara News-Press

The Gonzalez Adobe could be seen with the undeveloped Riviera in the background, circa 1900. Two architectural traditions, adobe and Victorian, existed side-by-side in Santa Barbara. Courtesy Santa Barbara City Library

The great American Santa Barbara residence predating the 1925 earthquake was the Dibblee Castle which stood on the hill overlooking the town on the site of the present-day SBCC campus. Thomas Bloodgood Dibblee (1823-1895) was a rancher and "sheep king" who married into the de la Guerra family. The mansion was built in 1882 and destroyed by the 1925 earthquake. Courtesy Santa Barbara Historical Society

Believe it or not, the University Club building once looked like this. It was originally built as a residence in 1880, but by 1922 it was considered a "Victorian horror" and converted into the Hispanic style building we have today. Photos courtesy UCSB Department of Special Collections and Santa Barbara News-Press

The Eisenberg Building, an interesting pre-1925 structure, stood at 1000 State Street. Courtesy UCSB Department of Special Collections

This photograph shows a damaged adobe with the old Sloyd School in background. The 1925 earthquake opened up the door for an Hispanic architecture that turned out to be based more on a style of buildings found in Spain than in nineteenth century-adobe Santa Barbara. Courtesy UCSB Department of Special Collections

The Plans and Planting Committee, a branch of the Community Arts Association founded in the 1920s, became the vehicle after the 1925 earthquake for creating what has been called a "New Spain in Santa Barbara." Led by Bernhard and Irene Hoffmann and Pearl Chase, and working in concert with the city's Architectural Board of Review, the committee was instrumental in the rebuilding of Santa Barbara in the Hispanic style of architecture. This photo is of a Plans and Planting Committee meeting in 1945. Courtesy UCSB Department of Special Collections

Architect James Osborne Craig (1889-1922), a Scotsman who spent childhood summers in Andalusia, designed El Paseo, among Santa Barbara's most important architectural treasures. Craig died before the complex of shops and apartments was opened in 1923. El Paseo became one of the models for rebuilding the town after the earthquake. Courtesy Santa Barbara Trust for Historic Preservation

El Paseo as seen at night in the 1920s. Courtesy Santa Barbara Historical Society

An early photograph of El Paseo's famous "Street in Spain." Courtesy Santa Barbara Historical Society

Among the most gifted architects working in Santa Barbara in the 1920s was George Washington Smith. Buildings he designed included the Lobero Theatre, the News-Press building, and the Little Town Club on Carrillo Street. This photo is an interior shot of Smith's Montecito home. Courtesy UCSB Department of Special Collections

There have been three different courthouses on the block bounded by Anacapa, Figueroa, Santa Barbara, and Anapamu streets. The first was made of adobe; the second, shown in this photo, was built in 1875 and destroyed by the 1925 earthquake. Courtesy Santa Barbara Public Library

The last of the three courthouses was completed in 1929. It is a building that Don Quixote could have designed: an utterly romanticized collection of styles as well as a hodgepodge of architectural elements, the courthouse is more than the sum of its parts. One architectural historian has described it as among the most beautiful buildings in the world. Courtesy Santa Barbara News-Press

Although this interior shot of the courthouse was made in 1974, its unchanging beauty could have been captured at any time. Courtesy Santa Barbara News-Press

Even the courthouse light fixtures are in keeping with its Mediterranean design. Courtesy Santa Barbara News-Press

This row of buildings along Figueroa Street is quintessential Santa Barbara architecture. Courtesy Santa Barbara Trust for Historic Preservation

The aesthetic charm and simplicity of Hispanic architecture are manifested in this archway at the corner of Victoria and Anacapa streets. Courtesy Santa Barbara Trust for Historic Preservation

Santa Barbara Junior High School (below), and Senior High School (right), both built in the 1930s, are two of the most beautiful public schools to be found anywhere. Photos courtesy Santa Barbara Trust for Historic Preservation and Santa Barbara News-Press

The romanticism implicit in the triumph of Hispanic architecture is reflected in this 1920s photo at El Paseo. The alternative to a Spanish revival could have been a town rebuilt on Bauhaus ideas. When one considers the architectural boxes made of glass, steel, and concrete that took over American cities in the 1930s, Santa Barbarans should indeed count themselves among the fortunate. Courtesy Santa Barbara Historical Society

Father Maynard Geiger, O.F.M., (1901-1977) served for years as archivist at the Old Mission and carried on the tradition of scholarly research begun by Father Zephyrin Engelhardt. A leading authority on Spanish colonial history, he authored The Life and Times of Junipero Serra, *and helped set up the Mission Archive, an invaluable repository of early California documents. Courtesy Santa Barbara* News-Press

Chapter Eight

The Southcoast's Creative Impulse

> The man that hath no music in himself,
> Nor is not mov'd with concord of sweet sounds,
> Is fit for treasons, strategems and spoils;
> The motions of his spirit are dull as night,
> And his affections dark as Erebus.
> Let no such man be trusted.—Mark the music.
> *The Merchant of Venice*

Let us "Mark the music" with Santa Barbara and examine the southcoast's creative impulse. The cognoscenti point to Ancient Greece and Renaissance Italy as pinnacles of cultural and intellectual achievement. How does Santa Barbara stack up in comparison to these places? In one way very similar—the arts and intellectual activity have in all three cases been nurtured by a wealthy class. A few pretentious panegyrists might go on to proclaim Santa Barbara equal to the others in creative output, but that's carrying it a bit too far.

Considering its size, however, Santa Barbara does have a remarkably rich cultural heritage. The region got off to a good start in the twentieth century thanks to the magnanimity of Montecito moguls who provided seed funding for the Santa Barbara Museum of Art, Museum of Natural History, Botanic Garden, Historical Society Museum, and Music Academy of the West.

One example will illustrate how a wealthy person can make a huge difference in the cultural life of a town. In the early twentieth century a member of the Board of Directors of the Carnegie Foundation stayed at the Potter Hotel and eventually built a home in Santa Barbara. Not long after, the Santa Barbara Community Arts Association received a large grant from that same foundation funding the arts in Santa Barbara for a number of years. The Community Arts Association in turn attracted a number of artists in the 1920s such as Ed Borein, Colin Campbell Cooper, Dudley Carpenter, and Clarence Mattei, to name just a few.

Two other important artists in the cultural history of Santa Barbara are Alexander Harmer, who came here early in the twentieth century and painted many authentic scenes of early Santa Barbara before his death in the twenties, and Ray Strong, who is still creating marvelous landscapes of the region. These two may not have the reputation of some of the other artists mentioned above, but their work seems more inspired by and in tune with the Santa Barbara surroundings.

A list of the fictional writers and poets who have touched the Santa Barbara soil would be endless. For most of them, Santa Barbara has been more a place of escape than inspiration. There have been, too, dozens of histories written on the region, the best known of which are the works of Walker Tompkins. These have been written for local consumption and not had much appeal to readers outside Santa Barbara. Among the novelists who spent considerable time here, the most talented have been Stewart Edward White and Ross Macdonald. Yet to appear on the scene is a major literary figure such as John Steinbeck or a major poet such as Robinson Jeffers. Nor despite a lively music and theatre performance tradition at the Music Academy of the West and the Lobero Theatre, has Santa Barbara become the springboard for a major dramatist or composer. But there's still plenty of time.

Today the University of California at Santa Barbara is the wellspring of much of the region's creative impulse. In the sciences and humanities is a gold mine of talent that has remained pretty much unknown outside the campus. Stronger ties between UCSB and the community could result in a cultural and intellectual energy of enormous proportions.

German-born Franciscan priest Zephyrin Engelhardt (1851-1934) worked for decades at the Old Mission researching and writing a history of the Franciscans in California entitled Missions and Missionaries of California *(four volumes). He also authored individual histories of most of the missions. While his works were written with a Franciscan bias, they contain a wealth of information. Courtesy Santa Barbara Historical Society*

Novelist Stewart Edward White (1873-1946) summered in Santa Barbara as a youth and moved here in 1903. According to one account, he left Santa Barbara in 1916 to escape the incessant flow of tourists trying to get a glimpse of the author in his home on the upper east side near the Mission. Well written, albeit sentimental in tone, his novel, The Rose Dawn *(1920), is a story about the town of Santa Barbara (called "Arguello" in the novel) coming to the rescue of Colonel Peyton (patterned in part after W. W. Hollister), who is about to lose his ranch to an east coast developer. Another one of his novels,* Ranchero (1933)*, contains vivid and accurate descriptions of life in California during the Mexican period. At the end of his life he began writing books on the occult. Courtesy Santa Barbara Historical Society*

Santa Barbara author Edwin Corle (1906-1956) with his wife, Jean, and their daughter. Among more than a dozen histories and novels, Corle's best known books are Royal Highway *and* Fig Tree John. *The latter book, a story about cultural conflict set at the Salton Sea, is one of the most powerful Indian novels ever written. At the time of his death, he was working on "The Californians," an epic novel set in Spanish Santa Barbara. The 2,400 page unfinished manuscript was never published. Courtesy Santa Barbara Historical Society*

Mystery writers Margaret Millar and Kenneth Millar (a.k.a. Ross Macdonald) on a bike ride through Hope Ranch in 1972. Becoming Santa Barbara residents in 1946, the authors pursued their own independent writing careers, publishing between them over fifty books. In 1982 Kenneth Millar died tragically, a victim of Alzheimer's Disease. Often compared with the best of the California mystery writers, Millar used Santa Barbara as the backdrop in several of his works, most notably in The Underground Man *(1971). Margaret Millar, featured recently in a* News-Press *article, also is a highly respected author and has continued writing and publishing since her husband's death. Photo by Rafael Maldonando; Courtesy Santa Barbara* News-Press

From the late nineteenth century to the present, scores of writers, poets and intellectuals have come to Santa Barbara, but usually only for brief visits. One example of this was a visit by Bertrand Russell (sitting) and Aldous Huxley in the 1930s. They had come with their wives for a brief vacation at the San Ysidro Ranch. Courtesy Santa Barbara Historical Society

In 1958 novelist Aldous Huxley, at left, returned to Santa Barbara to give a series of lectures at UCSB. While there, University of California President Clark Kerr presented him with an honorary doctorate, the first given at UCSB. Huxley worked on his novel Island *during his year in Santa Barbara. Courtesy George and Vivian Obern*

Nobel Prize winning novelist Sinclair Lewis (1885-1951) paid a visit to Santa Barbara in 1947. Courtesy Santa Barbara News-Press

Henry Chapman Ford (1828-94) came to Santa Barbara in 1875 and became the town's first full-fledged artist resident. His painting of the Santa Barbara Mission is on the dustcover of this book. Courtesy Santa Barbara Historical Society

A remarkable number of historical accounts on Santa Barbara have been written from the end of the nineteenth century to the present. Walker Tompkins, pictured here, one of the most prolific local history writers, has authored over a dozen works and until recently was heard daily on his radio show "Santa Barbara Yesterdays." Courtesy Santa Barbara News-Press

After spending a few years painting the Southwest during a stint in the army in the 1880s, Alexander Harmer (1856-1925) came to Santa Barbara and married Felicidad Abadie, a descendant of an early California family. He then proceeded to paint authentic scenes of early California, which he meticulously researched before executing. Charles Fletcher Lummis wrote of him: "No other painter has given so much attention to California of the old times and for that matter no other painter knows the subject one-half so well." Courtesy Santa Barbara News-Press

This scene of a dance at Casa de la Guerra is typical of the fine work of Harmer. Courtesy Santa Barbara News-Press

Herbert Bayer is considered among the most influential figures in twentieth-century art and design. He was trained at the Bauhaus, an experimental art school founded in 1919 by Walter Gropius in Germany. Bayer lived in Santa Barbara during the last decade of his life in the 1970s and 1980s and completed hundreds of art works. The Bauhaus movement has had very little impact on Santa Barbara art and architecture, with one exception: A large chromatic gate designed by Bayer is soon to be installed on park land between Calle Puerta Vallarta and Cabrillo Boulevard. Courtesy Santa Barbara News-Press *and William Dewey*

More than sixty years ago Santa Barbara was the center of the motion picture industry. Opened in 1910 at the corner of State and Mission streets, the Flying A Studio became the largest of its kind in the world. Mostly Westerns were produced there, and over twelve hundred movies were made before the studio was phased out in 1921. D. W. Griffith was the most famous name to have worked there. Courtesy Santa Barbara Historical Society

An aerial view of the Flying A Studio. Courtesy Santa Barbara Historical Society

On the set of Buck Parvin of the Movies, *produced at the Flying A Studio. Courtesy Santa Barbara* News-Press

Jose Lobero was the man who built the original Lobero Theatre. Soon after the theatre was opened, Lobero suffered financial reverses and was forced to sell out. Despondent, he shot himself. Courtesy Santa Barbara News-Press

Dating from 1873, the Lobero Theatre is one of Santa Barbara's oldest and most important cultural institutions. It became the cultural and social center of nineteenth-century Santa Barbara, with the small problem that it was located in the slum part of town. In fact, an old fire map refers to the area around the theatre as "Nigger Alley." Courtesy Santa Barbara Historical Society

The interior of the old Lobero Theatre. Courtesy Santa Barbara News-Press

The new Lobero Theatre, opened in 1923, continues to provide fine music and theatre productions, lectures and more. Courtesy Santa Barbara Trust for Historic Preservation

In recent years, a seven-hundred seat festival theatre has opened in Solvang. A New York drama critic has hailed it as "One of the finest of its kind in the country." Courtesy Santa Barbara News-Press

The world famous German opera star Lotte Lehmann arrived in Santa Barbara a refugee from Hitler's Germany. She had been asked by Hermann Goering to become the Diva of Nazi Germany. When she fled to the United States, the Nazis executed her dog. In Santa Barbara she settled into her home in Hope Ranch, where she lived for the rest of her life. She pursued a brilliant teaching career at the Music Academy of the West. In this photograph, Lehmann (left) watched as her prize pupil Grace Bumbry (middle) sang at the academy in 1957. Courtesy Santa Barbara News-Press

The old post office at Anapamu and State streets became the Santa Barbara Museum of Art in 1937. It is one of a number of creative institutions that have grown out of the fertile Santa Barbara cultural soil. Courtesy Santa Barbara Historical Society

Spencer Kellogg donated his Montecito home in 1944 to the Vedanta Society of Southern California. The society established an ashrama there which became the Sarada Convent. Adjoining it, the temple was designed by Lutah Maria Riggs to resemble a temple of southern India and was completed in 1956. Daily vespers, classes, and lectures gather a community of students and worshippers before portraits of Jesus, Buddha, and Ramakrishna in the Temple. Vedanta, an ancient Hindu philosophy based on the belief that God is the underlying reality of every being, teaches respect for all religions. Courtesy Vedanta Society of Southern California

Swamis of the Ramakrishna Order in the United States gathered in Montecito in 1947 to celebrate the first formal monastic vows in the West of their order. Swami Prabhavananda, founder of the Vedanta Society of Southern California, is in the foreground. Courtesy Vedanta Society of Southern California

The prime movers behind the Historical Society in the 1950s and 1960s were Andriette and Edwin Gledhill. Edwin also contributed mightily to the creation of the Pueblo Viejo historical district in downtown Santa Barbara. Courtesy Santa Barbara Historical Society

The Center for the Study of Democratic Institutions was the brainchild of Robert M. Hutchins, shown here with J. Cogley in 1968. The Center opened in 1959 ensconced in the old Peabody Mansion on Eucalyptus Hill. Plagued by financial problems and coming under attack from the "Old Right" and the "New Left," the Center was forced to sell off its property and move to the University. The goal of "great minds" discussing "great issues" did not last. Said Hutchins of the Center: "I used to say of the University of Chicago that it was not a very good university; it was just the best there was. The truth about the Center... is that it is not a very good center, but it's the only one there is." Courtesy Santa Barbara News-Press

In 1891 the Sloyd School opened in the 800 block of Santa Barbara Street. It specialized in the so-called manual arts. By 1906 teacher training was added. A few years later Governor Hiram Johnson agreed to appropriate $10,000 if a new site was found. The campus was moved to the Riviera in 1915. By 1935 it was upgraded to a State College with a full liberal arts program and a new campus site at Leadbetter Hill. *Courtesy Santa Barbara* News-Press

Pictured here is a typical Sloyd School class room where boys learned manual arts; girls were taught home economics. Courtesy Santa Barbara News-Press

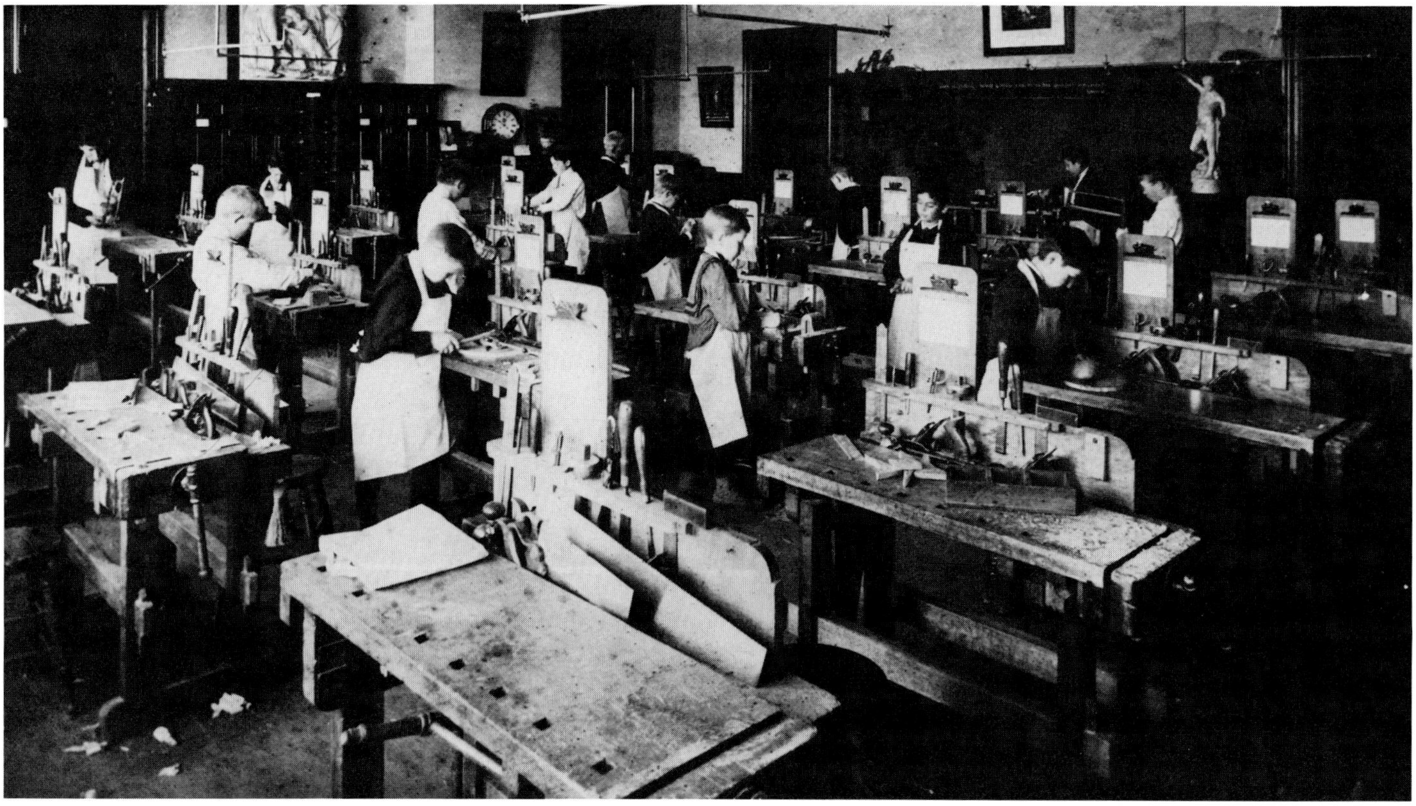

In the 1950s the Air Force took over old Camp Cooke, turned it into a missile testing site and renamed it Vandenberg Air Force Base. Unique coastal geography, allowing polar-orbit launches over the ocean, made it a site the Air Force wanted. Discoverer I, the first polar-orbited satellite, was launched from Vandenberg in 1958. The photo is of a firing of an Atlas ICBM in the 1960s. Courtesy Santa Barbara Historical Society

A Minuteman missile test at Vandenberg in 1980. Courtesy Santa Barbara News-Press

In the 1970s hopes were high as planning and construction began for the Shuttle launch at Vandenberg. This 1976 drawing is of a Space Shuttle launch. Courtesy United States Air Force

In 1979 two Air Force generals compared a Space Shuttle launch site rendering with actual work underway in the background. Since the Shuttle tragedy in 1986, the program at Vandenberg has been put on hold. In fact, it appears that it will remain in mothballs, with the site possibly used for launching S.D.I. ("Star Wars") satellites. Courtesy United States Air Force

Not everyone in Santa Barbara is pleased with the military presence in the county, as witnessed by these protesters at Vandenberg Air Force Base in 1983. Courtesy Santa Barbara News-Press

The military has a major economic impact on Santa Barbara County, especially in Goleta where a number of companies depend upon military contracts. Defense-related industries provide at least a third of the jobs available in the county. Raytheon, a defense-dependent contractor and one of the largest employers in Santa Barbara, is seen in this aerial photograph from 1967. Courtesy Santa Barbara News-Press

These workers at the Raytheon plant seem intent on their labors. Courtesy Santa Barbara News-Press

In 1981 five iron cannon encrusted with tar were found exposed at Goleta Beach after a storm. They have become the subject of an intense historical debate. One theory of their origin suggested the cannon might have been Francis Drake's and that the Goleta Slough might be the long sought after site of Drake's landing in California in 1579. A more plausible hypothesis is that these are the cannon abandoned during a rebellion of Monterey Presidio soldiers who marched to Santa Barbara in the 1830s. Photo by Steve Malone; Courtesy Santa Barbara News-Press

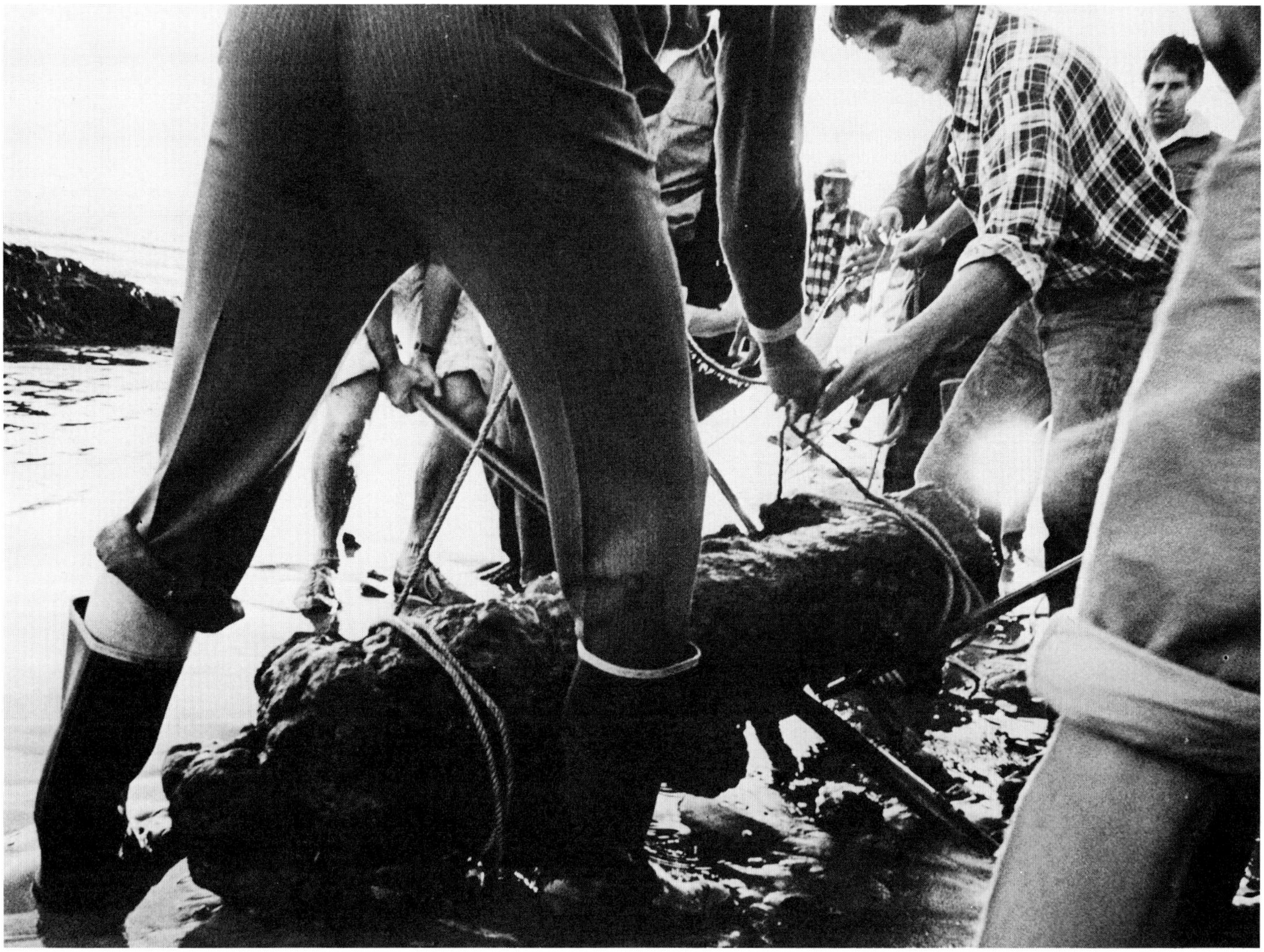

Dr. J. Walter Collinge, a Santa Barbara Historical Society volunteer, and archaeologist Dr. Pandora Snethkamp both took special interest in the restoration of the cannon. The cannon are now on loan to the Goleta Valley Historical Society under a cooperative agreement between the Goleta Valley and Santa Barbara Historical societies, the Santa Barbara Trust for Historic Preservation, and the county. Photo by Doug Pensinger; Courtesy Santa Barbara News-Press

Sailing is one of the pleasures of the Santa Barbara lifestyle. Courtesy Santa Barbara News-Press

Chapter Ten

The Sybaritic Santa Barbara Lifestyle

Santa Barbara has the reputation of being one of the pleasure paradises of the world. This image dates from 1872 when Charles Nordhoff, paid by a railroad company to prepare a guide titled "California for the Traveler and Health Seeker," waxed enthusiastic about the region as one of the most pleasant places in California. This brought the first wave of leisure and pleasure seekers; a steady stream has been coming ever since.

After the sun-starved, pasty tourist has been here a while, he becomes one of the tanned "brown" people. On weekends and summer days, the wharf and beaches are crowded with visitors and locals all participating to the fullest in the activities of leisure: swimming; body, board, and wind surfing; playing volleyball; frisbee-chasing with friend or dog; scuba diving; sailing; and fishing. On land it's jogging, running, bicycling, roller skating, and skate boarding, and at home, it's barbecue and "bubbles" (hot tubbing) time, in the land where the hot tub originated in the early 1970s.

Some Santa Barbarans may object to this image of their town, but it's the one the average visitor takes away with him. For the locals, the Santa Barbara lifestyle is more myth than reality, because as year-round residents, they know it's not all milk and honey—that the high cost of real estate makes living here a struggle to survive. There is often talk of Santa Barbara becoming only a playground for the affluent, although in truth it's been pretty much just such a place since the turn of the century. The middle class has always had a tough go of it here.

In the late 1960s and early 1970s the so-called alternative hippie or communal life-style emerged, the most memorable group being the "Brotherhood of the Sun." The alternative lifestyle was also found in Isla Vista, which to some was, and still is, a student ghetto. But again the high cost of real estate has intervened to render this life-style infeasible, unless one chooses to join the band of homeless roaming the streets.

From inside Santa Barbara, it is easy to react cynically to the reality of trying to eke out a living in "Lotus Land," but there are enough rewards for most people to make the struggle worthwhile. The Fiesta or party tradition of Santa Barbara dates back to Spanish times and remains part of the enjoyment of living and playing in this land of the lovely climate and beautiful scenery.

To outsiders, especially from the East Coast, the Santa Barbara mode of living and the California notion of "getting in touch with one's feelings" seem outrageously decadent and self-indulgent. But hedonism is what Santa Barbara is all about, and a host of local denizens and vacationers undoubtedly will continue to pursue it with a vengeance in the years ahead.

Stearns Wharf, built in 1872, as it appeared in the 1890s before the development of Cabrillo Boulevard and arrival of the lively beachfront world that today attracts sun seekers in droves. Courtesy UCSB Department of Special Collections

This aerial view shows the coastline from downtown out to Goleta. The beautiful beaches and salubrious climate are the essence of the Santa Barbara Lifestyle. Courtesy Santa Barbara News-Press

Sunday strollers at the beach, circa 1903, with the nearly completed Potter Hotel in the background. Courtesy UCSB Department of Special Collections

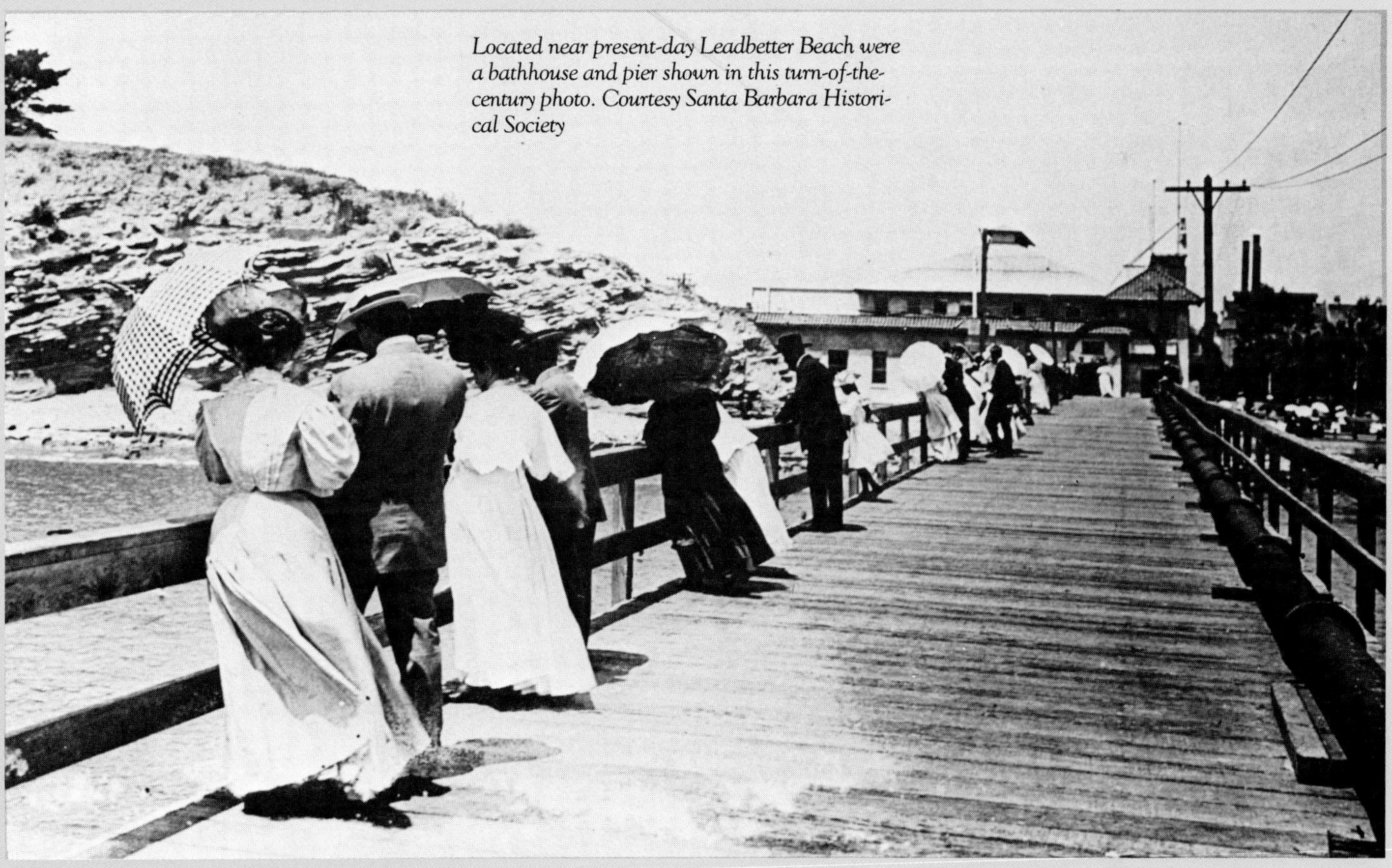

Located near present-day Leadbetter Beach were a bathhouse and pier shown in this turn-of-the-century photo. Courtesy Santa Barbara Historical Society

From the turn of the century to the present, children playing at the beach has been one of Santa Barbara's most enduring traditions. Courtesy UCSB Department of Special Collections

Victorian women strolled the beach fully clothed at the turn of the century, while the modern woman feels quite comfortable in her bikini enjoying a game of volleyball. Photo by Steve Malone; Courtesy Santa Barbara News-Press

Surfing off Coral Casino. Photo by Steve Malone; Courtesy Santa Barbara News-Press

On a clear day with a view of the surrounding mountains it is hard to deny that this is paradise. This photo was taken in the 1930s. Courtesy Santa Barbara News-Press

The lure of the sun was too much for these UCSB students in the early 1960s. It's a "problem" every generation of UCSB students faces. Courtesy UCSB Department of Special Collections

Among the hotels catering to weathy sunseekers was "Samarkand," which was opened in 1921. Built in a Persian architectural style, it was known mostly for its beautiful terraced gardens. The hotel has been converted into a retirement home. Courtesy Santa Barbara News-Press

The world of the hot tub looms large in the Santa Barbara lifestyle. In fact, Santa Barbara is where the hot tub originated. Courtesy Noel Young, Capra Press

A group of Santa Barbarans rest at La Cumbre Peak in the early twentieth century. The occasion was the dedication of the recently completed trail from the town up to the peak, an event that marked the opening of the Santa Ynez Mountains backcountry. While the beach life is what is identified as most typical of the Santa Barbara lifestyle, a unique backcountry laced with a network of trails has become a place to escape the hectic pace of urban life. Courtesy Santa Barbara News-Press

Dr. James G. Mills and his son Jimmy paused along the Sisquoc River in 1965. Their hike took them through areas now under Congressional protection as the San Rafael and Dick Smith wildernesses. Dr. Mills, a leading authority on gray whales, past-president of the local Audubon Society, and a member of the Sierra Club, is an example of a citizen committed to preservation and protection of the environment for the enjoyment of future generations. Courtesy Santa Barbara Museum of Natural History

Isla Vista, or "I.V." as it is called by those who live there, has been a unique Santa Barbara "institution" for decades. It's where the young college student reigns supreme and where the lifestyle, according to one mailbox in the 1960s, is based on "love." Courtesy UCSB Department of Special Collections

Young people have drifted in and out of I.V. over the years. Hippies in the 1960s found the place to their liking. In this photo three boys commune with the sidewalk. Courtesy UCSB Department of Special Collections

Enjoying a park in I.V., "a jug of wine, and thou." Courtesy UCSB Department of Special Collections

The Brotherhood of the Sun, founded in 1969 by Norman Paulsen, was a back-to-nature, semi-Christian, semi-meditation group. Initially living on a ranch off Gibraltar Road, the Brotherhood later expanded to other sites and took over Gaviota Village in 1978. A communal society, members turned all of their money and possessions over to their church. Courtesy Santa Barbara News-Press

The Brotherhood opened up vegetable and fruit stores that turned healthy profits. It all came unglued in 1981, when some members moved out of Santa Barbara and others filed suit against leader Paulsen. Photo by Rafael Maldonado; Courtesy Santa Barbara News-Press

A strong strain of the Santa Barbara lifestyle is the fiesta spirit. From the nineteenth-century celebrations at Casa de la Guerra to the El Paseo Restaurante parties of the twentieth century, Santa Barbarans have always been ready to have a good time. Courtesy Santa Barbara Trust for Historic Preservation

Santa Barbara is renowned for its annual Old Spanish Days celebration—a summertime festival of parades and entertainment at various sites around town. The highlight of the events is the historical parade. Courtesy Santa Barbara Historical Society

Storke's proudest accomplishment was helping obtain federal funding for construction of the Cachuma (Bradbury) Dam in the 1950s. The dam solved Santa Barbara's water problem into the 1970s. But today the issue of an insufficient water supply is once again a problem with which the county must grapple. Courtesy Santa Barbara News-Press

For the most part, Santa Barbara politics have had a distinctive local flavor, but this photo of a Ku Klux Klan rally in 1923 evidences the fact that national political currents could make their way into town. Courtesy Santa Barbara News-Press

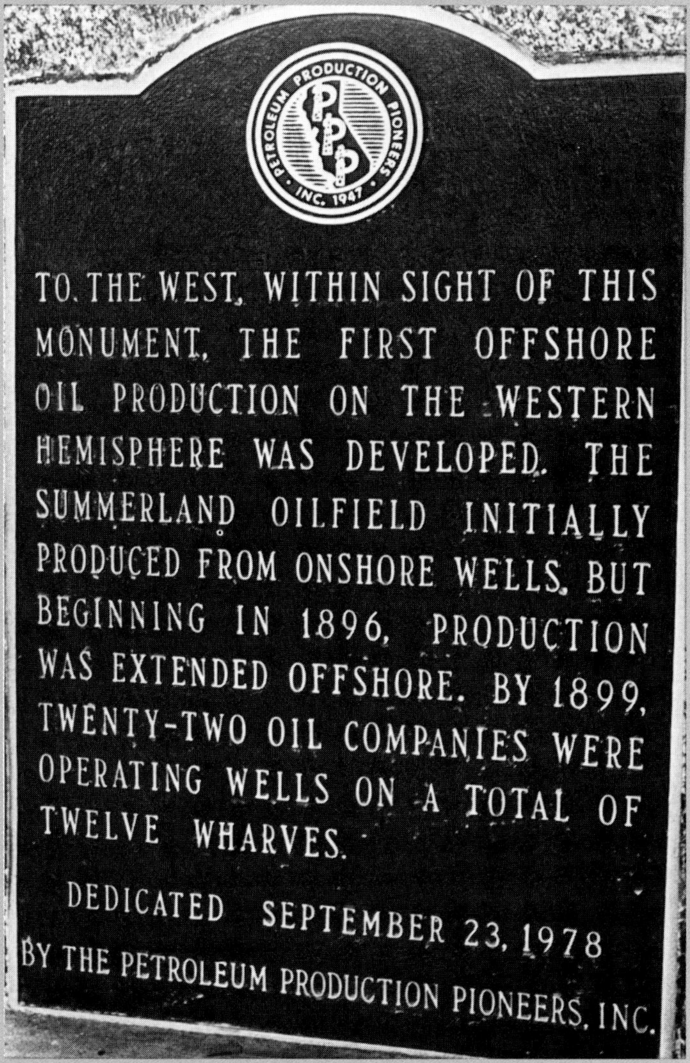

This plaque in Summerland speaks for itself. In an earlier time, oil derricks in Summerland and on the Mesa were a common sight. Courtesy Santa Barbara News-Press

The Beach at Summerland looked like this around 1910. Courtesy Santa Barbara News-Press

Sailboat enthusiasts sail past the oil derricks on the mesa. Courtesy Santa Barbara Historical Society

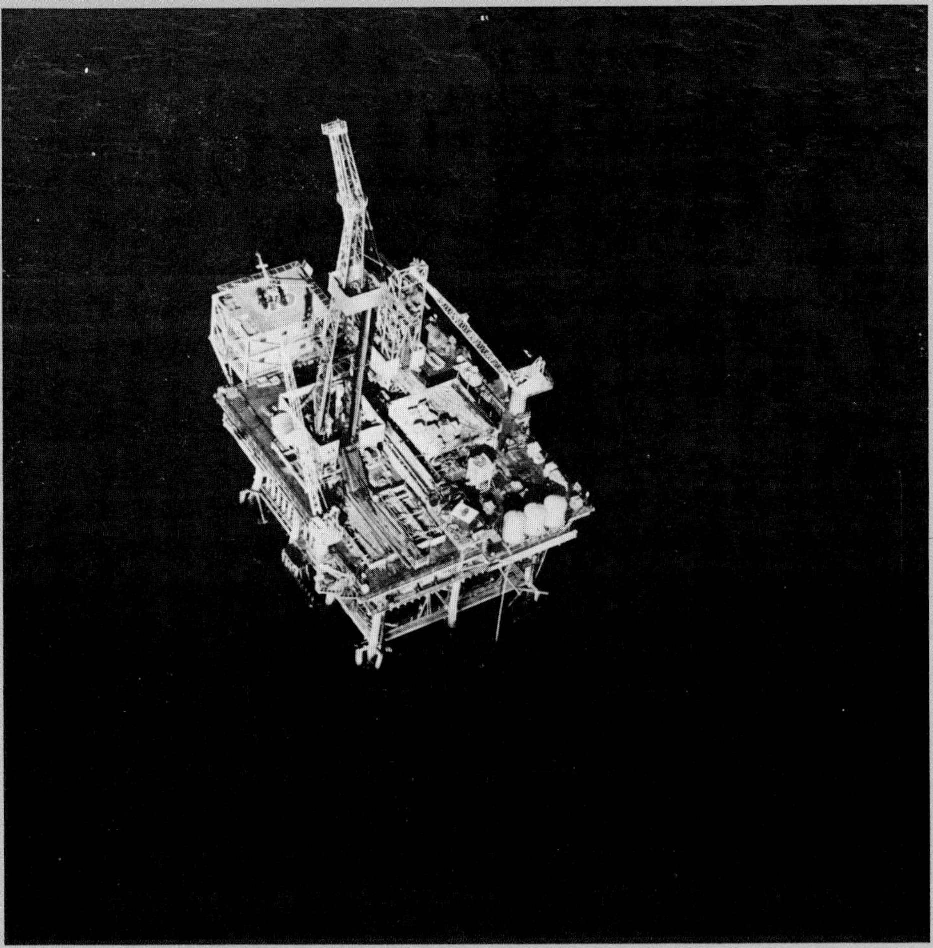

There was a false sense of security as offshore oil development expanded in the 1960s, but in 1969 a Union Oil well ruptured and hundreds of thousands of gallons of oil were released into the channel. Mystery novelist Ross Macdonald wrote in one of his books that the oil platform "stood up out of its windward end like a dagger that had stabbed the world and made it spill black blood." Courtesy Santa Barbara News-Press

The oil spill-blackened beaches were among the first signs of problems to come. Courtesy Santa Barbara News-Press

The "black tide" drifted into the harbor as workers frantically worked to clean up the mess. Courtesy Santa Barbara News-Press

Stations were set up to clean oil-covered birds. In the background directly behind the bird, then-State Senator Robert Lagomarsino looked on. Courtesy Santa Barbara News-Press

Police were called in to break up a sit-in protest against Union Oil at Stearns Wharf. Courtesy Santa Barbara News-Press

Angry Santa Barbarans formed G.O.O. after the spill and for a few years were able to limit offshore oil development. Then came the first OPEC-engineered oil crisis and Santa Barbara's environmental concerns bowed to the nation's energy needs. Oil platforms have proliferated in the channel in the last decade. Courtesy Santa Barbara News-Press

Dick Smith, long-time News-Press *reporter, was among those deeply upset by the spill. An environmental consciousness that emerged in Santa Barbara out of the oil spill spread across the nation. Courtesy Santa Barbara* News-Press

A life-long fighter for environmental causes, Dick Smith had a wilderness area in the Santa Ynez Mountains named after him. Sierra Club member Ann Van Tyne, Susan Soria (Smith's daughter), and Congressman Robert Lagomarsino were at the wilderness dedication ceremony in 1987. Courtesy Santa Barbara News-Press

The 1960s will be most remembered as a time of racial upheaval and protest against the Vietnam War. On April 4, 1968, Martin Luther King was assassinated and mourners marched down State Street in memory of their lost leader. Courtesy Santa Barbara News-Press

In 1969 and 1970, Isla Vista turned into a maelstrom of war protest that culminated in the burning of the Bank of America. Local police and the Los Angeles County Sheriff Department were called in to enforce a curfew. Arrests and violence ensued, with dozens of students injured in the melee. Then a UCSB student, attempting to get the rioters to calm down, was killed by a bullet of unknown origin. Kevin Moran's death brought the I.V. riots to a screeching halt. A sardonic poster appeared in I.V. stores showing the Bank of America on fire. Courtesy UCSB Department of Special Collections

Protests also took place in downtown Santa Barbara. In a 1972 march up State Street, long-haired students yelled out profanities and epithets in a desperate attempt to get the attention of the "Establishment." Courtesy Santa Barbara News-Press

In the late 1970s politics in Santa Barbara returned to local issues. Most important to Santa Barbarans was finding a way to prevent unbridled growth á la Los Angeles. By 1965 traffic on State Street, as seen in this photograph, was already becoming a problem. Removing parking helped improve the situation, but traffic and parking are problems that remain in 1988. Courtesy Santa Barbara News-Press

In an attempt to revitalize the downtown, the city pushed forward plans in 1982 to allow development of a department store on the site of this book store. The owners of Earthling, in concert with other shopkeepers and Santa Barbara residents, got an initiative on the ballot, and the project was voted down. The City Redevelopment Agency moved down the street and proposed another department store project about twice the size of the original. It has been approved with only mild protest. Courtesy Santa Barbara News-Press

In the future, as they have been in the past two decades, county-wide growth and the attendant threat to the quality of life will be the central political issues for Santa Barbarans. This photo is of Las Palmas Drive in the early days of the Hope Ranch development. Courtesy Santa Barbara Historical Society

An aerial view looking out toward Goleta in 1962 demonstrates how much growth Santa Barbara has undergone in the past twenty-five years. Both sides of the freeway are now covered by residential development. Environmentalists have used the water issue as a way to limit growth, but as California's population continues to swell, Santa Barbara will feel the inevitable pressure to take its fair share. Courtesy Santa Barbara News-Press

Mayoral politics have been fairly tame in the twentieth century with one exception: in 1934 Edmund O. Hanson was elected mayor on a reform ticket. Upon taking office, he fired almost all of the city's department heads and soon was feuding with the City Council. He survived a recall, but after being cited for contempt of court by a judge he had engaged in battle, he decided discretion was the better part of valor and resigned in 1936. Courtesy Santa Barbara News-Press

Three of Santa Barbara's most distinguished mayors, John Rickard (1953-57), Sheila Lodge (1982 to present), and Patrick Maher (1936-45), posed for this photo in 1984 at the annual meeting of the Santa Barbara Trust for Historic Preservation. After two two-year terms as mayor, Rickard went on to become a superior court judge (1968-82); Patrick Maher, who served as mayor when the position had considerably more power under the city charter, remained a respected Santa Barbara citizen until his death at ninety-eight in 1986. Sheila Lodge is Santa Barbara's first woman mayor. Photo by William B. Dewey

Bibliography

Anderson, Eugene N. *The Chumash Indians of Southern California.* Banning, California: Malki Museum Press, 1968.

Bancroft, Hubert Howe. *History of California.* Vol. I (1542-1800), Vol. II (1801-1824), Vol. III (1825-1840). San Francisco: History Company Publishers, 1886.

Beilharz, Edwin A. *Felipe de Neve. First Governor of California.* San Francisco: California Historical Society, 1971.

Benson, Arlene and Bob Edberg. "On the Road to Goleta," *Journal of California and Great Basin Anthropology,* Vol. IV, No. 2 (1982), 288-295.

Bente, Vance, Judith Tordoff, and Mary Hillerman-Smith. *Phase VIII Archaeological Investigations of the Chapel Site.* Santa Barbara: Santa Barbara Trust for Historic Preservation, 1982.

Blackburn, Thomas C., ed. *December's Child: A Book of Chumash Oral Narratives Collected by John Peabody Harrington.* Berkeley, California: University of California Press, 1975.

Bookspan, Rochelle, ed. *Santa Barbara by the Sea.* Santa Barbara: McNally and Loftin, 1982.

California's Chumash Indians. Santa Barbara: John Daniel Publishers, 1986.

The California Missions: A Pictorial History. (A Sunset Book) Menlo Park, California: Lane Publishing Company, 1979.

Camarillo, Albert. *Chicanos in a Changing Society from Mexican Pueblos to American Barrios in Santa Barbara and Southern California 1848-1930.* Cambridge, Mass.: Harvard University Press, 1979.

Callaghan, Catherine A. "J. P. Harrington—California's Great Linguist," *Journal of California Anthropology.* Vol. II, No. 2 (1975) 183-187.

Conrad, Rebecca, and Christopher H. Nelson. *A Guide to Pueblo Viejo.* Santa Barbara: Capra Press, 1986.

Corle, Edwin. *Fig Tree John.* New York: Liveright, 1971.

______. *The Royal Highway (El Camino Real).* New York: Bobbs-Merrill Company, 1949.

Dana, Richard Henry. *Two Years Before the Mast.* New York: Harper and Brothers, 1840.

Easton, Robert A. *The Black Tide. The Santa Barbara Oil Spill and its Consequences.* New York: Delacorte Press, 1972.

______. *This Promised Land. A Novel.* Santa Barbara: Capra Press, 1982.

Engelhardt, Zephyrin. *Mission Santa Ines Virgin Y Martir.* Santa Barbara: McNally and Loftin, 1986.

______. *The Missions and Missionaries of California.* Four Volumes. San Francisco: James H. Barry Company, 1915.

______. *Santa Barbara Mission.* San Francisco: James H. Barry Company, 1923.

Farley, Marco. "The Legacy of Pearl Chase." Unpublished Manuscript, 1987.

Gidney, C. M., Benjamin Brooks, and Edwin Sheridan. *History of Santa Barbara, and San Luis Obispo, and Ventura Counties, California.* Chicago: Lewis Publishing Company, 1917.

Hawley, Walter. *The Early Days of Santa Barbara, California.* New York: n.p., 1910.

Heizer, Robert F., ed. *California.* Volume VIII in William C. Sturtevant, general editor. *Handbook of North American Indians.* Washington, D.C.: Smithsonian Institution, 1978.

History of Santa Barbara County, California with Illustrations and Biographical Sketches of its Prominent Men and Pioneers. Oakland, California: Thompson and West, 1883.

"A History of the Santa Barbara Presidio Area from 1846 to the Present," Unpublished UCSB Public History Monograph.

"How did Santa Barbara get that way?" *Sunset.* (January 1975) 36-43.

Hudson, Travis, et. al., editors. *The Eye of the Flute: Chumash Traditional History and Ritual as told by Fernando Librado Kitsepawit to John P. Harrington.* 2nd Edition. Banning, California: Malki Museum Press, 1981.

James, Carollyn, "A Field Linguist who Lived his Life for his Subjects," *Smithsonian,* Vol. XV, No. 1 (April 1984) 153-174.

Keefe, Susan E., and Amado M. Padilla, *Chicano Ethnicity.* Albuquerque: University of New Mexico, 1987.

Kelsey, Harry. *Juan Rodriguez Cabrillo.* San Marino, California: Huntington Library, 1986.

Laird, Carobeth. *Encounter with an Angry God. Recollections of my Life with John Peabody Harrington.* Banning, California: Malki Museum Press, 1975.

Macdonald, Ross. *The Blue Hammer.* New York: Alfred A. Knopf, 1976.

______. *Self-Portrait. Ceaselessly into the Past.* Santa Barbara: Capra Press, 1981.

______. *Sleeping Beauty.* New York: Bantam Books, 1987.

______. *The Underground Man.* New York: Alfred A. Knopf, 1971.

McWilliams, Carey. *Southern California: An Island on the Land.* Salt Lake City: Peregrine Smith, Inc., 1973.

Neuerburg, Norman. *Eighteenth Century Santa Barbara Presidio Chapel Secrets Uncovered by Twentieth Century Research.* Foreword by Jarrell C. Jackman. Santa Barbara: Bellerophon Books, 1985.

Nordhoff, Charles. *California for Health, Pleasure, and Residence. A Book for Travelers and Settlers.* Unabridged Edition. Berkeley, California: Ten Speed Press, 1973.

O'Neill, Owen H., ed. *History of Santa Barbara County. Its People and Resources.* Santa Barbara: n.p., 1939.

Phillips, Michael James. *History of Santa Barbara County.* Two Volumes. San Francisco: S. J. Clarke Publishing, 1927.

Pickerell, G. Albert and Mary Dornin. *The University of California: A Pictorial History.* Berkeley University of California, 1968.

"Report of Santa Barbara Citizens' Commission on Civil Disorders. What Occurred? Causes? What Can and Ought to be Done?" Santa Barbara, California, September 15, 1970.

Robinson, Alfred. *Life in California.* Salt Lake City: Peregrine Publishers, 1970.

Ruhge, Justin. *Goleta. Pueblo de Las Islas.* Santa Barbara: Kimberly Press, 1984.

Santa Barbara. A Guide to the Channel City and its Environs. Compiled and written by the Southern California Writer's Project of Work Projects Administration. New York: Hastings House, 1941.

Sipper, Ralph, ed. *Inward Journey. Ross Macdonald.* Santa Barbara: Cordelia Editions, 1984.

Southworth, John R. *Santa Barbara and Montecito. Past and Present.* Santa Barbara: Schauer Printing, 1920.
Spaulding, Edward S. *Adobe Days along the Channel.* Santa Barbara: Schauer Printing. 1957.
Sterling, Clarence R., "Chumash Wind Instruments," *News From Native California.* Vol. II, No. 2 (May/June 1988) 4-8.
Stirling, M. W. "John Peabody Harrington 1884-1961." *American Anthropologist.* Vol. 65, No. 1 (1963) 370-381.
Storke, Thomas M., with Walker Tompkins. *California Editor.* Los Angeles: Westernlore Press, 1958.
Thompson, Joseph A. *El Gran Capitan. Jose de la Guerra.* Los Angeles: Cabrera and Sons, 1961.
Tompkins, Walker A. *Old Spanish Santa Barbara.* Illustrated by Russell Antonio Ruiz. Santa Barbara: McNally & Loftin, 1967.
———. *Santa Barbara History Makers.* Santa Barbara: McNally & Loftin, 1983.
Vancouver, George. *A Visit to the Santa Barbara Royal Presidio in 1793.* Santa Barbara: Bellerophon Books, 1986.
Weber, David J. *The Mexican Frontier 1821-1846. The American Southwest under Mexico.* Albuquerque: University of New Mexico Press, 1982.
White, Stewart Edward. *Ranchero.* New York: Doubleday Doran and Company, 1933.
———. *The Story of California. Gold (1903). The Gray Dawn (1915). The Rose Dawn (1920).* New York: Halcyon House, 1940.
Whitehead, Richard, ed. *An Archaeological and Restoration Study of Mission La Purisima Concepcion.* Santa Barbara: Santa Barbara Trust for Historic Preservation, 1980.
———, ed. *A Spanish Soldier in the Royal Presidio of Santa Barbara.* Translated by Jarrell C. Jackman. Santa Barbara: Bellerophon Books, 1987.
———, ed. *The Voyage of the Frigate Princessa to Southern California in 1782.* Translated by Geraldine V. Sahyun. Santa Barbara: Santa Barbara Mission Archive Library, 1982.

(Author's Note: In addition to the books, articles and unpublished materials listed above, I perused various issues of *Noticias,* the quarterly magazine of the Santa Barbara Historical Society, and a number of newspaper articles found in the *News-Press* clipping files.)

Index

About the Author

Jarrell C. Jackman is Executive Director of the Santa Barbara Trust for Historic Preservation, where he has worked since 1981. He majored in German at the University of California, Los Angeles, and holds an M.A. in American Studies from California State University, Los Angeles, and a Ph.D. in history from the University of California, Santa Barbara. After spending four years in Germany as an academic exchange research fellow and university history lecturer, he lived from 1978 to 1980 in Washington D.C. He co-edited and was a contributor to the Smithsonian Institution Press volume *The Muses Flee Hitler: Cultural Transfer and Adaptation 1930-45* (1983). Among his most recent publications is a translation of Rafael Gonzalez's *Experiences of a California Soldier.* At present he is at work on a book of poetry and on a biography of Presidio comandante Felipe de Goicoichea.